CROSSWORD

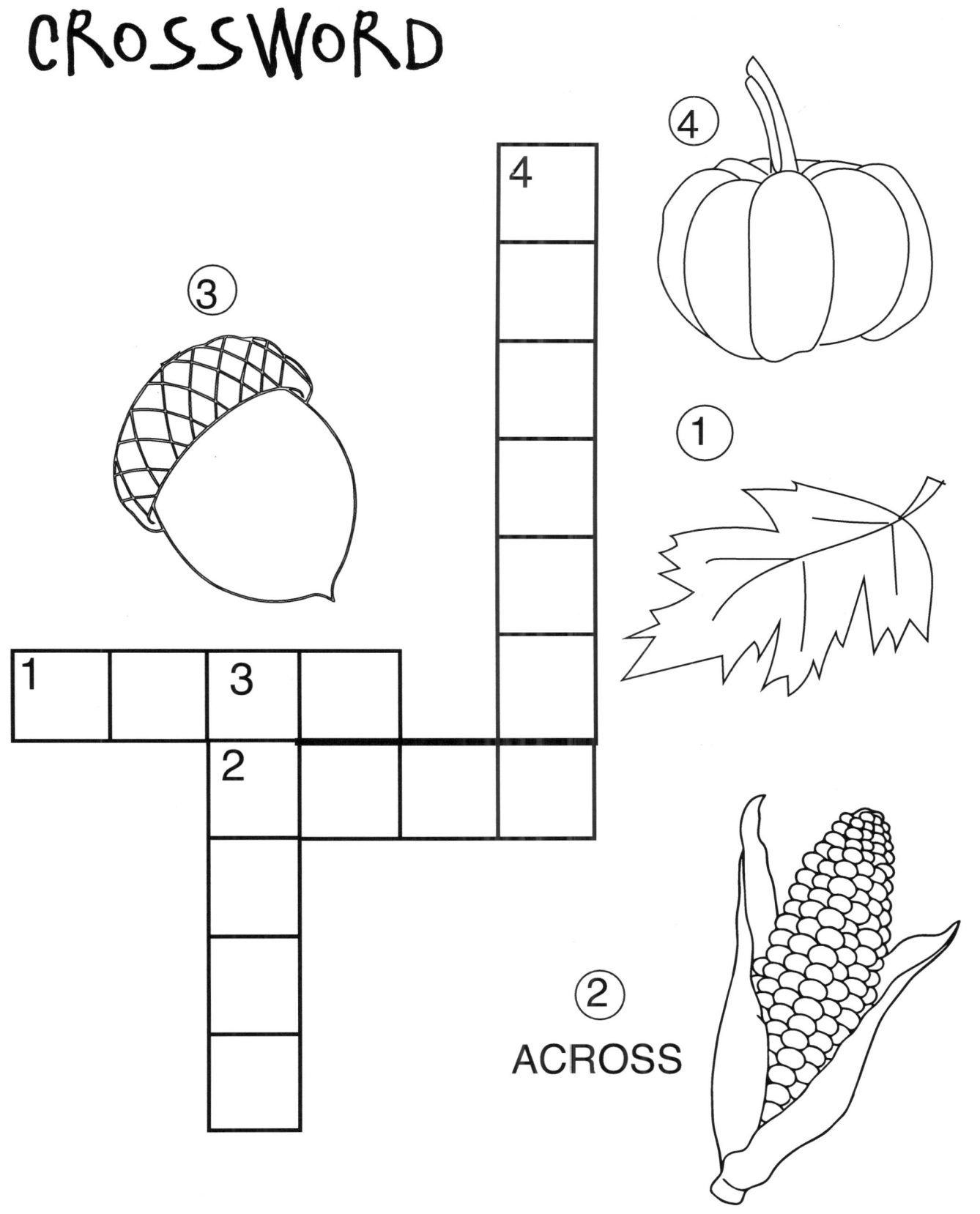

WRITE THE WORDS ASSOCIATED WITH THE PICTURES

ONE OF A KIND

FIND THE IMAGE THAT IS ONE OF A KIND

JOIN THE DOTS

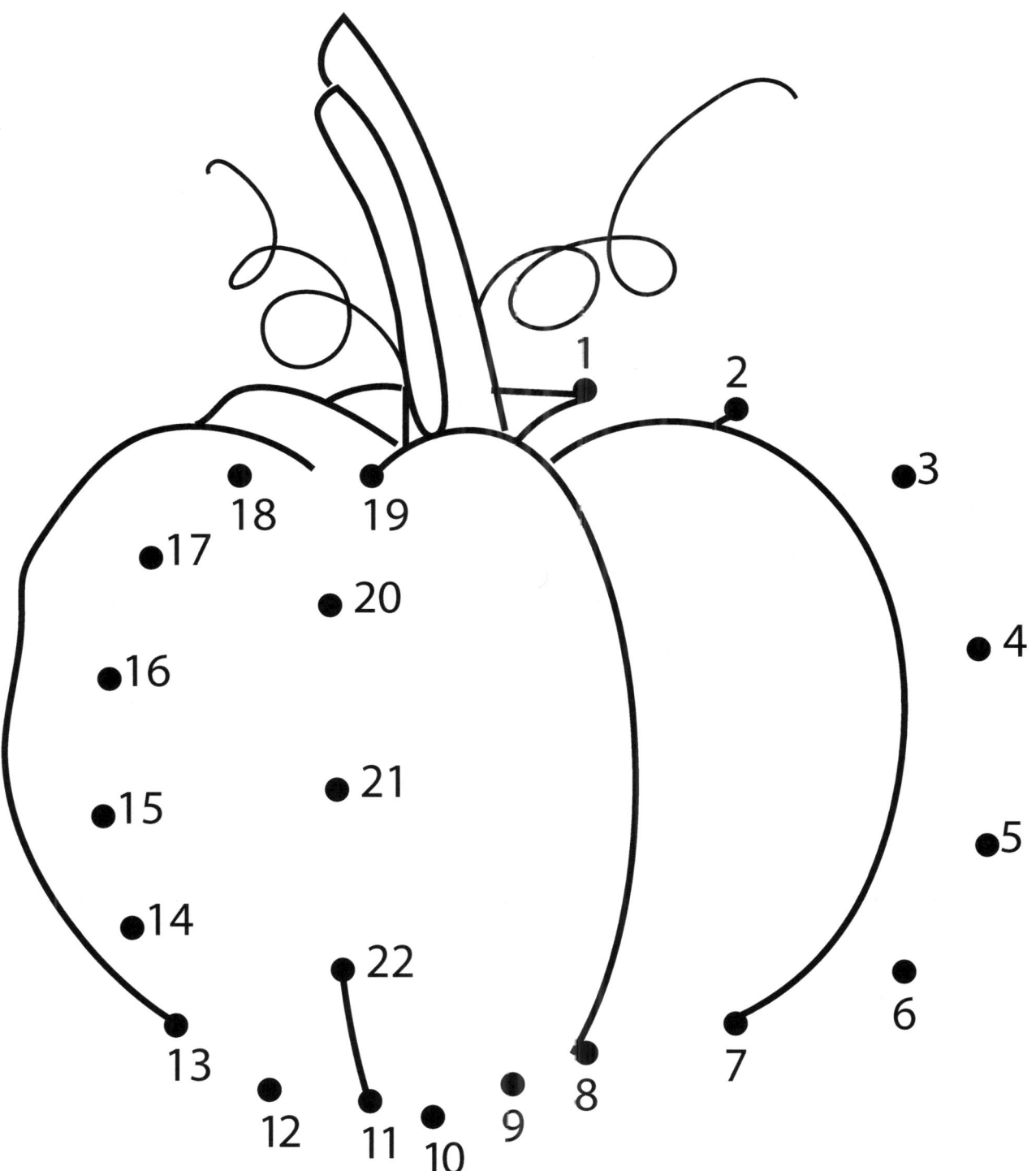

UNSCRAMBLE

ANORC   _ _ _ _ _

AEPPL   _ _ _ _ _

LVEAES   _ _ _ _ _ _

FLLA   _ _ _ _

CNRO   _ _ _ _

GRDOU   _ _ _ _ _

HVESTAR   _ _ _ _ _ _ _

CLOO   _ _ _ _

HYA   _ _ _

REARRANGE THE LETTERS IN THE CORRECT
ORDER TO FIND THINGS RELATED TO AUTUMN

COMPLETE THE PICTURE

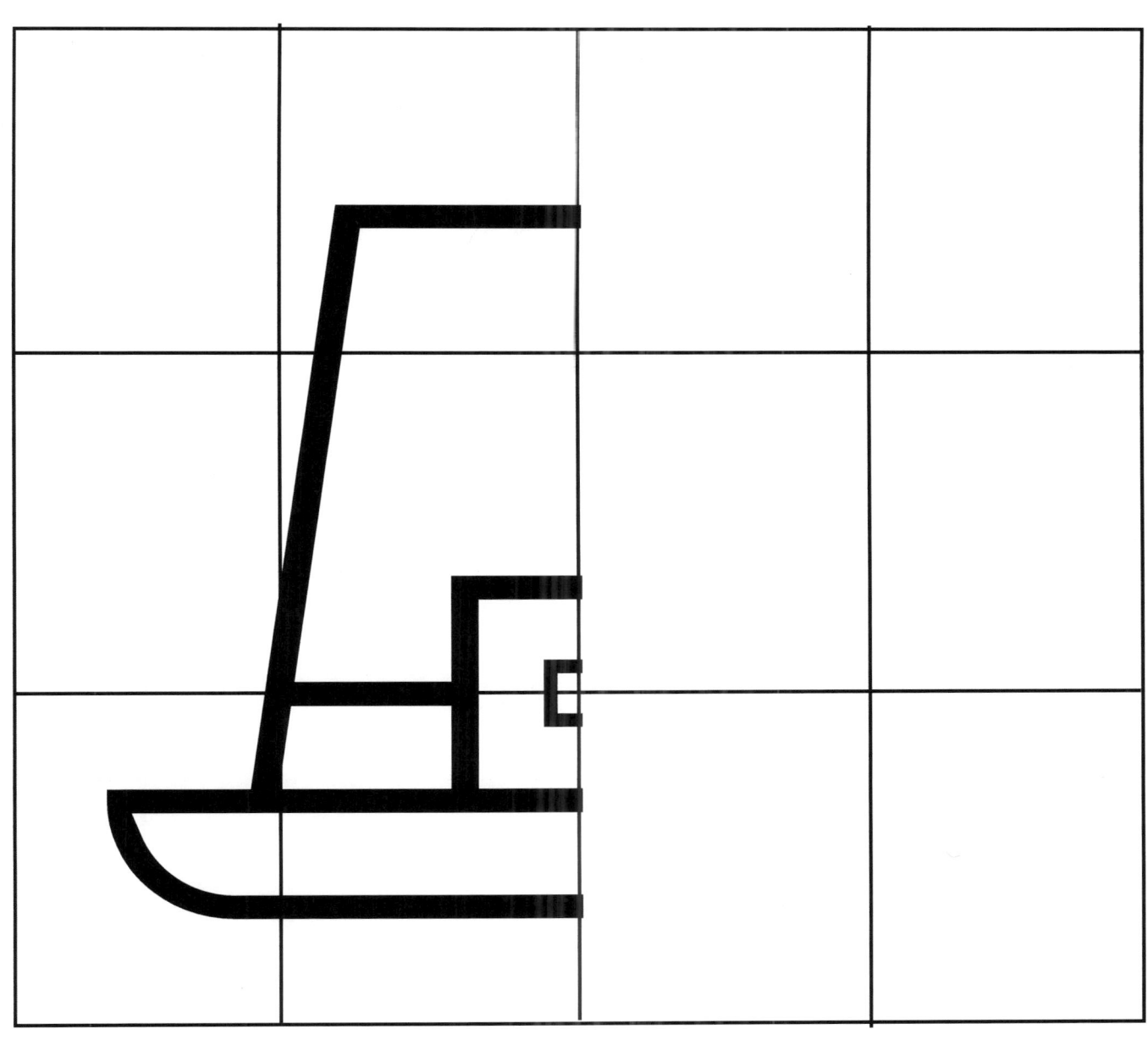

DRAW the OTHER HALF OF THE HAT
BY FOLLOWING THE GRID

COMPLETE THE PICTURE

DRAW the OTHER HALF OF THE PUMPKIN
BY FOLLOWING THE GRID

JOIN THE DOTS

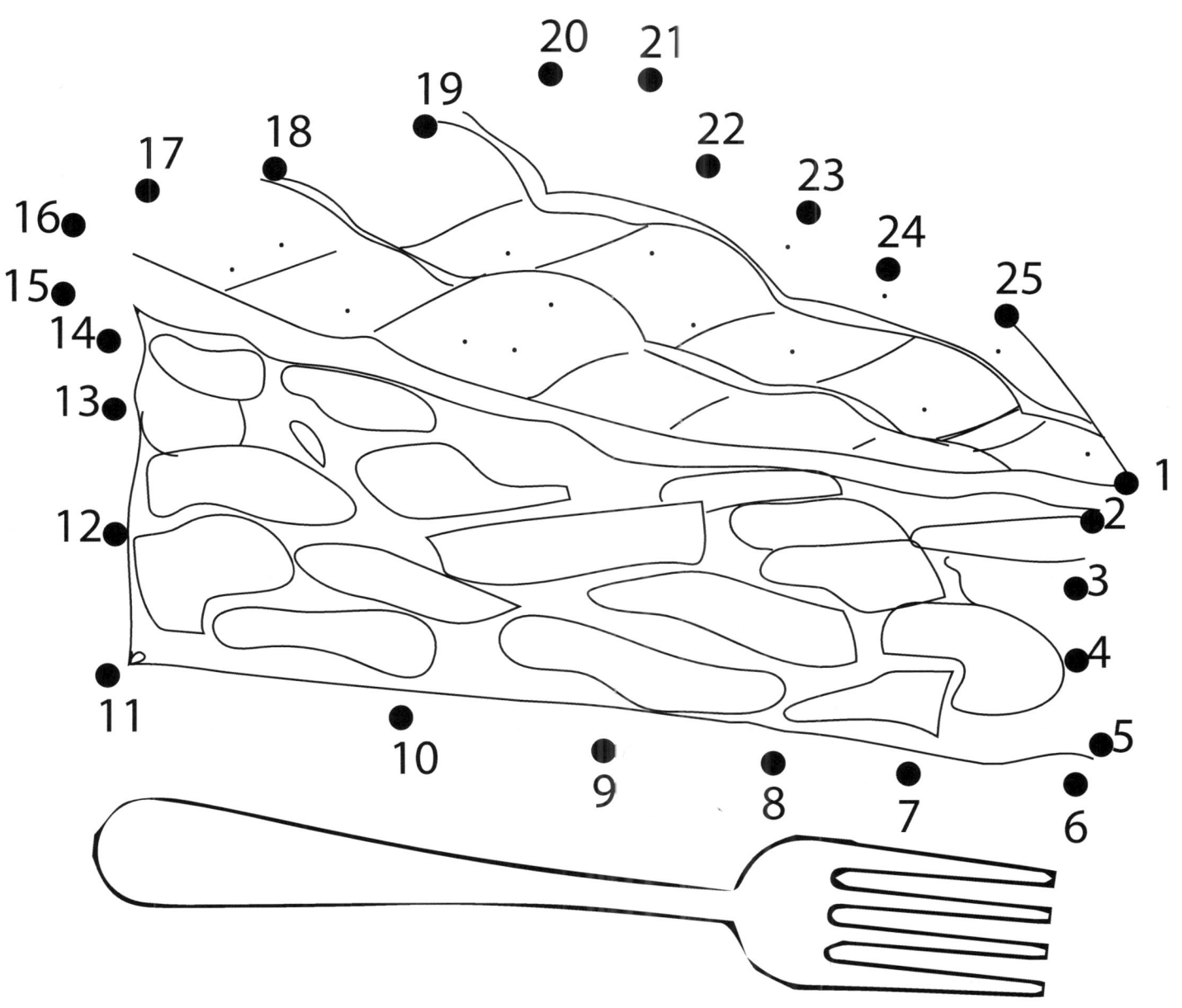

MATCH THE SHADOW

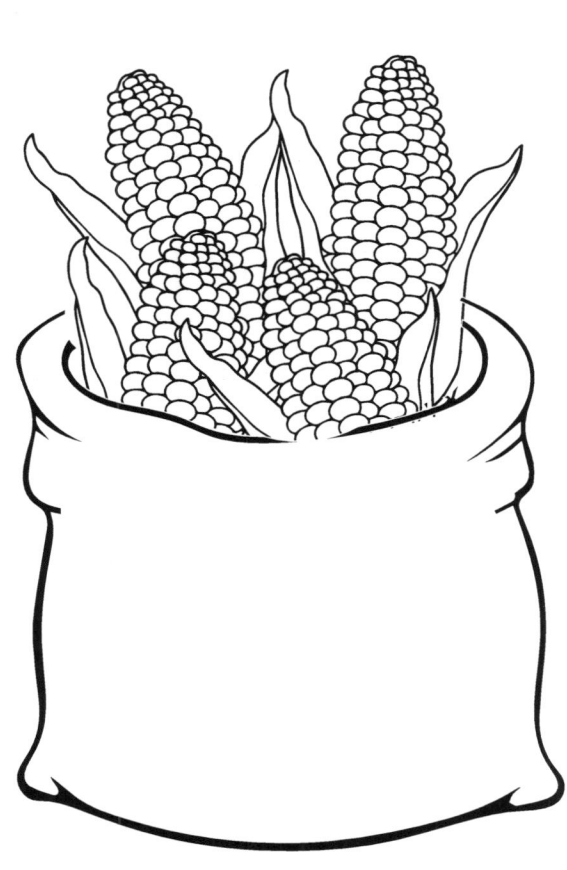

SELECT THE SHADOW
THAT MATCHES THE
SACK OF CORN

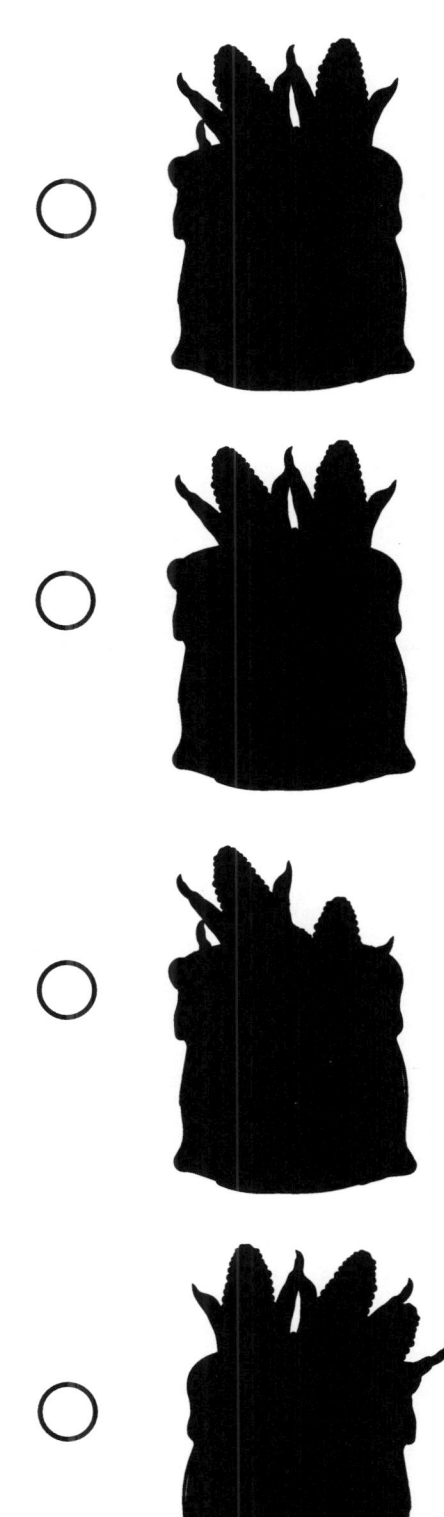

COMPLETE THE PICTURE

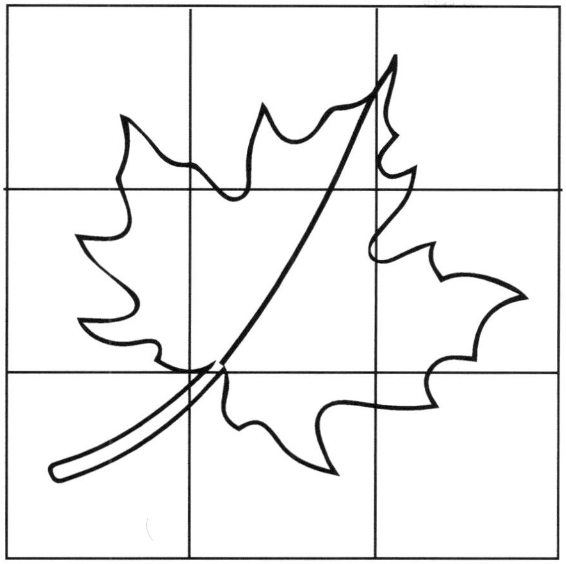

DRAW THE LEAF BY
FOLLOWING THE GRID

COMPLETE THE PATTERNS

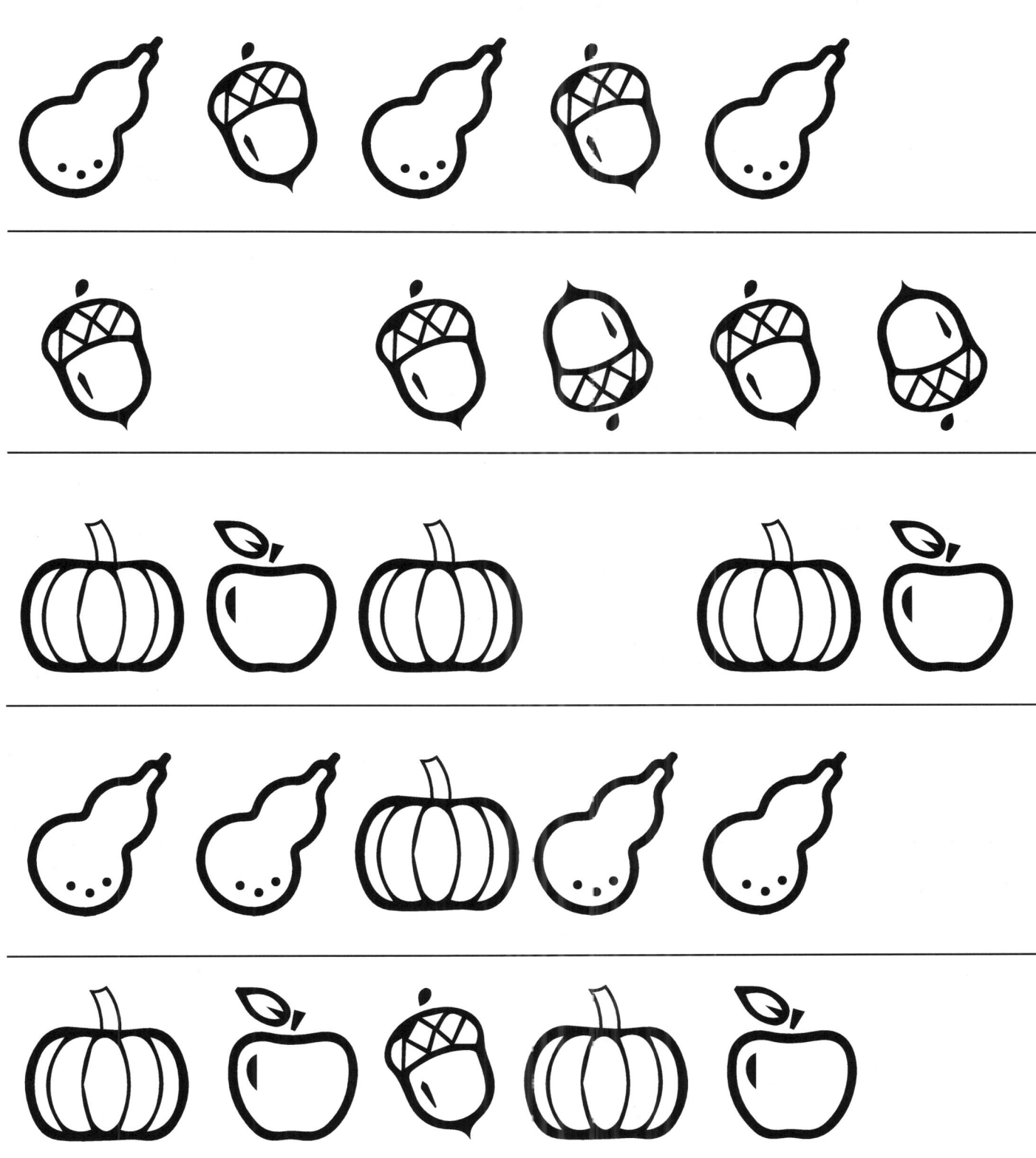

COMPLETE THE PATTERNS IN EACH ROW

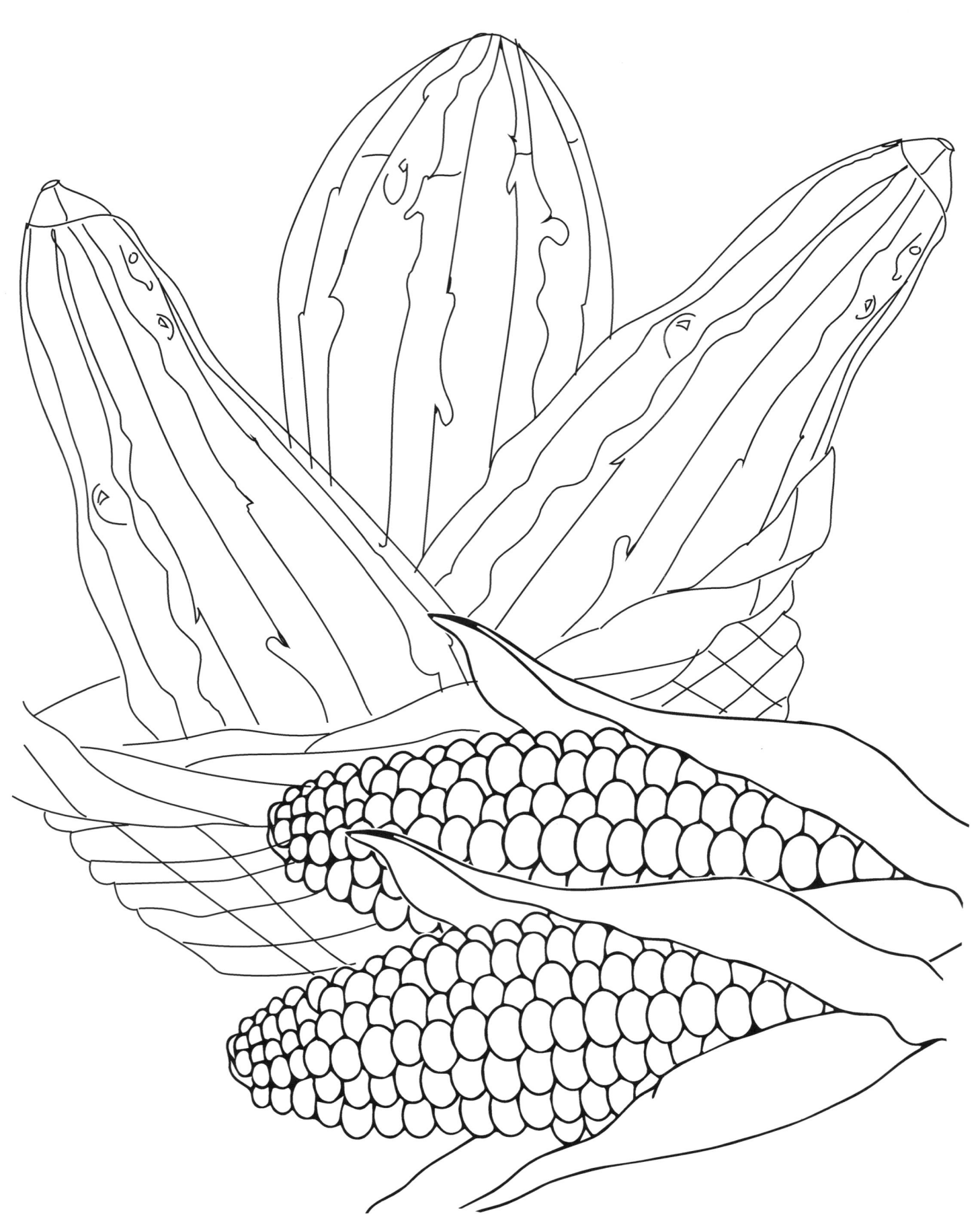

PLACE VALUE
CIRCLE THE NUMBER IN THE TENS PLACE

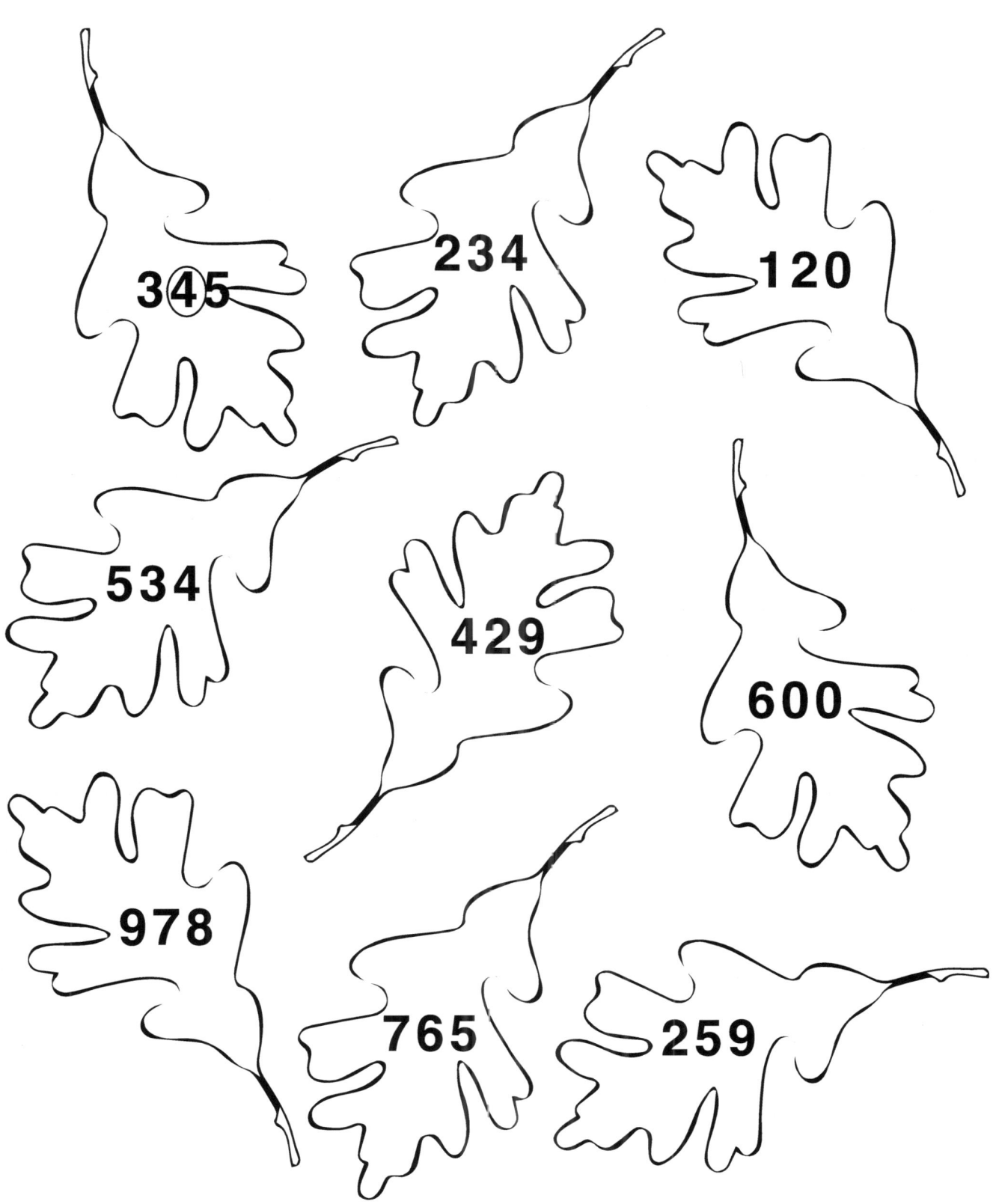

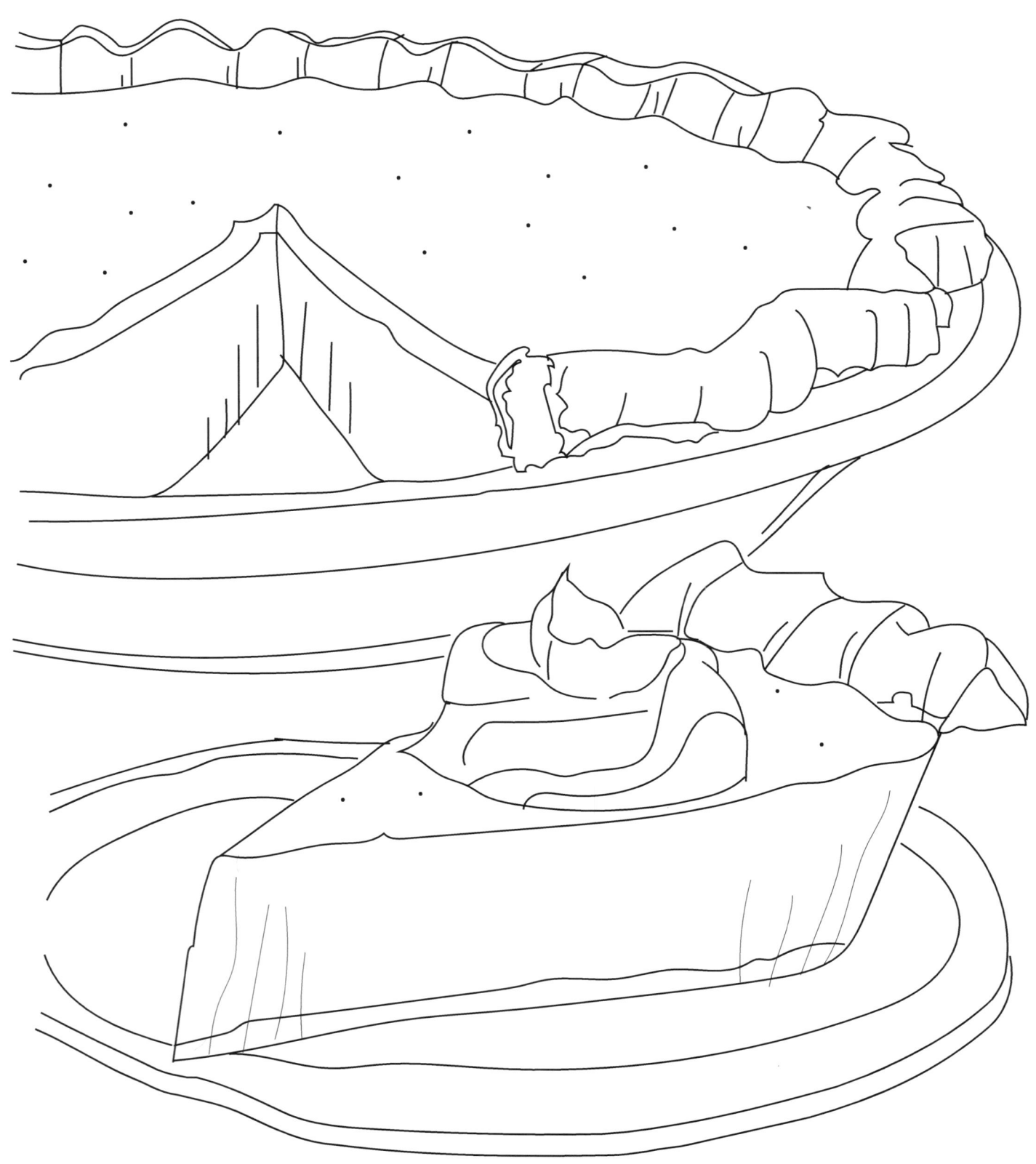

FIND THE tWINS

FIND AND CIRCLE THE TWO IDENTICAL LEAVES

COMPLETE THE PICTURE

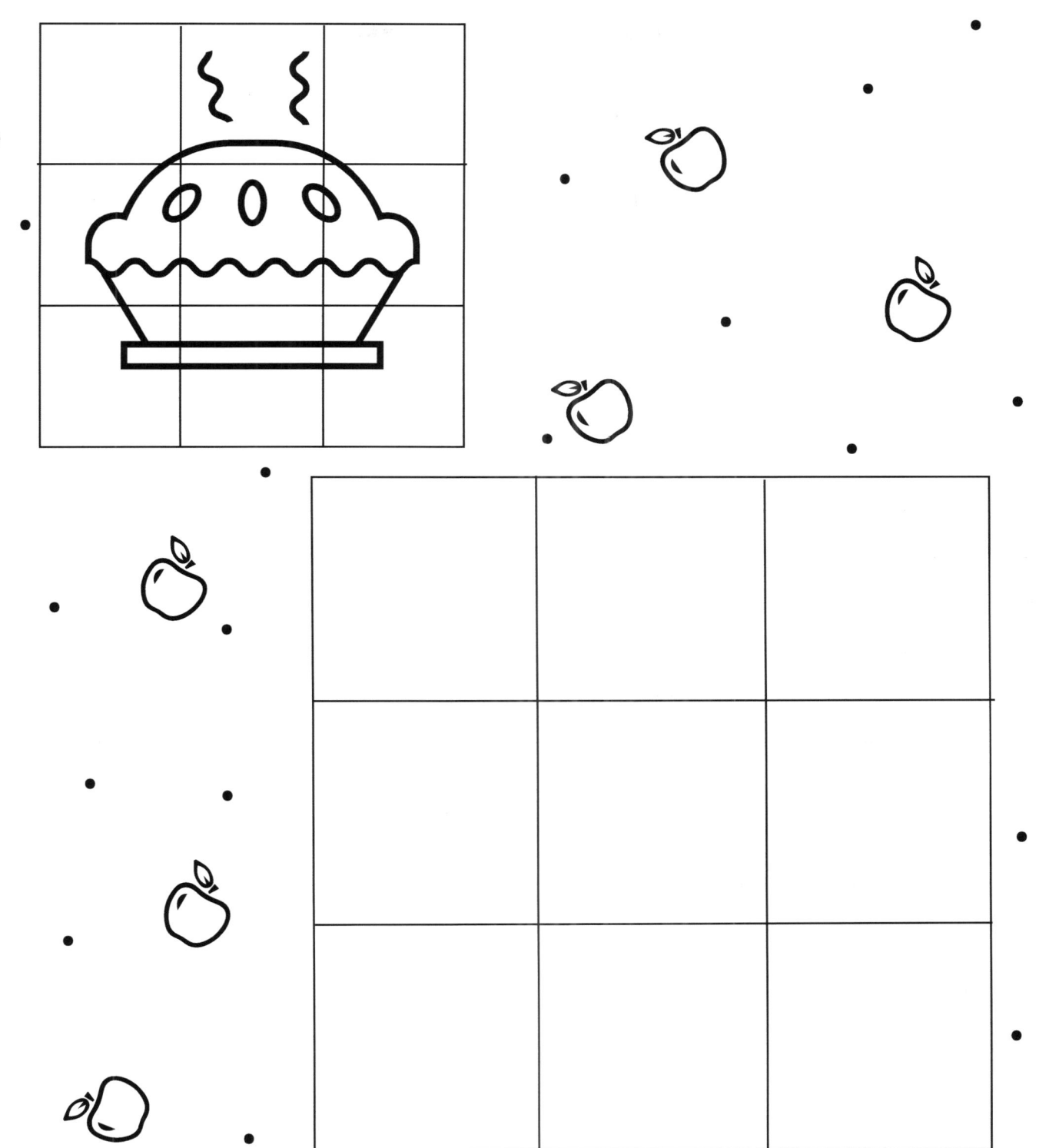

DRAW THE PIE BY
FOLLOWING THE GRID

MATCH THE FOLLOWING

RIPE   DOWN

HOT   RAW

UP   COLD

FALL   WINTER

SUMMER   RISE

MATCH THE OPPOSITE WORDS

COUNT AND WRITE

COUNT THE NUMBER OF LEFT AND RIGHT ACORNS

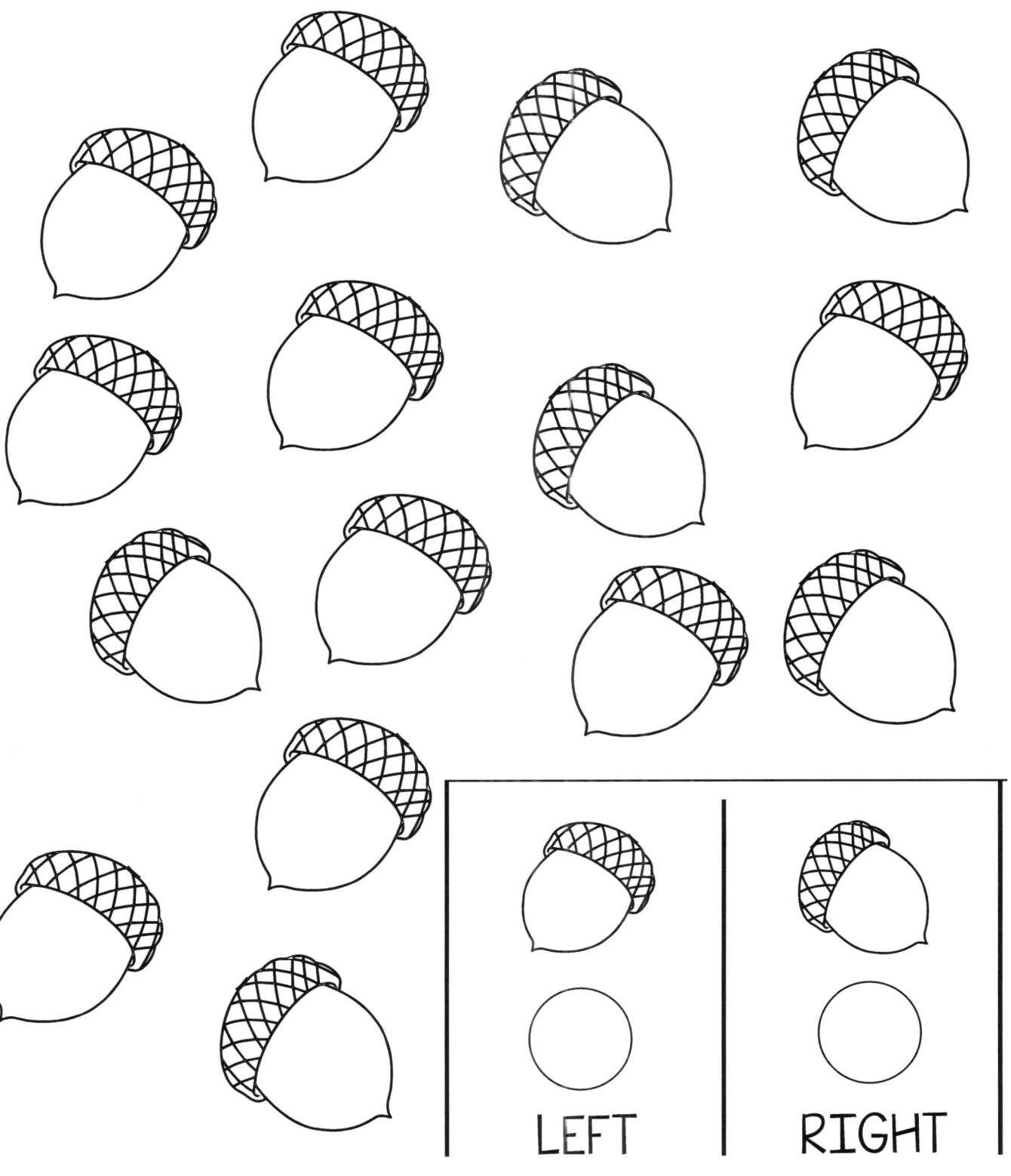

LEFT

RIGHT

MATCH THE FOLLOWING

MATCH THE PICTURES WITH THE AUTUMN FRUITS AND VEGETABLE

PUMPKIN

APPLE

ACORN

GOURD

LESS IS MORE

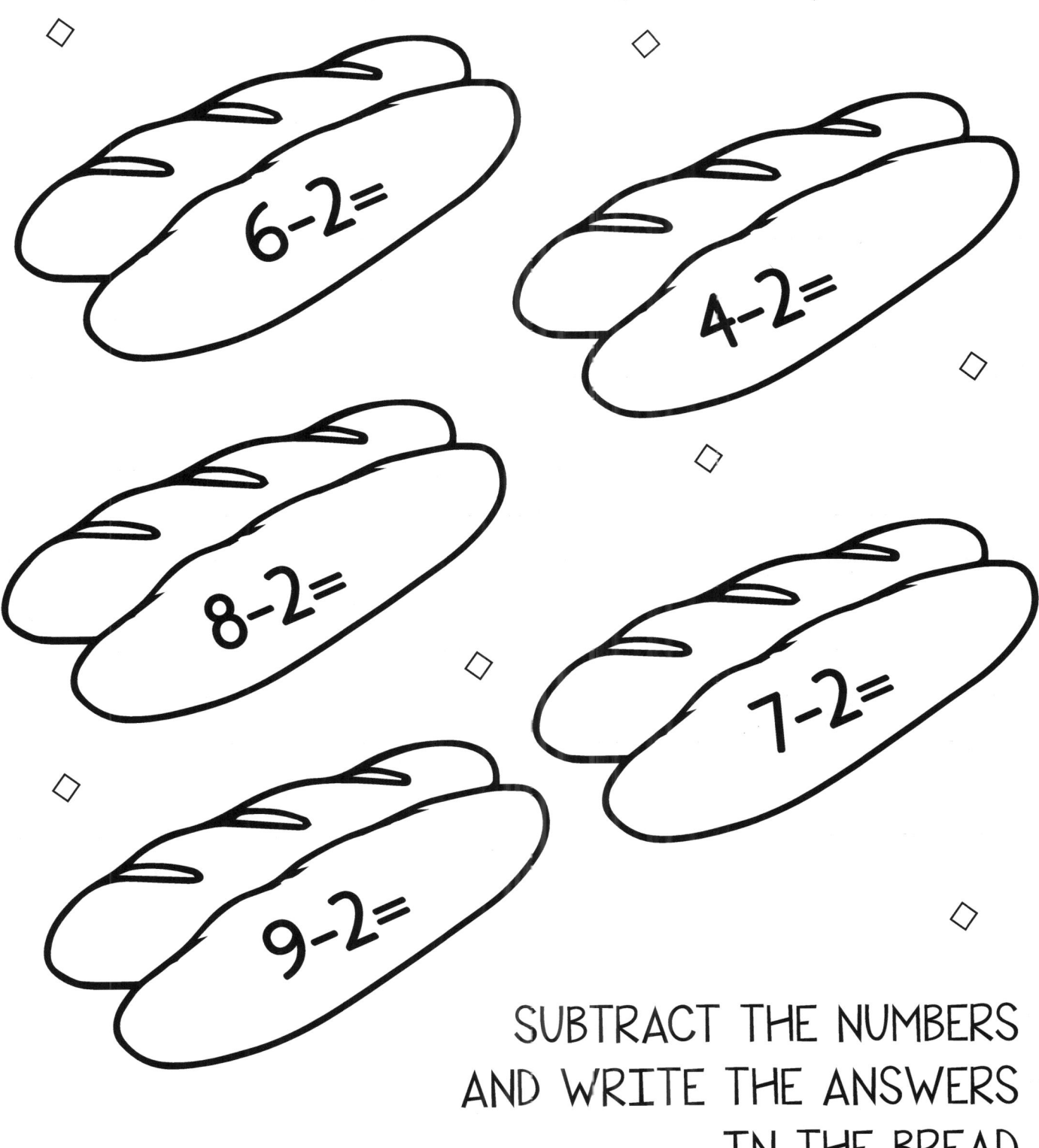

6-2=

4-2=

8-2=

7-2=

9-2=

SUBTRACT THE NUMBERS
AND WRITE THE ANSWERS
IN THE BREAD

LESS IS MORE

SUBTRACT THE NUMBERS AND WRITE
THE ANSWERS IN THE TURKEY

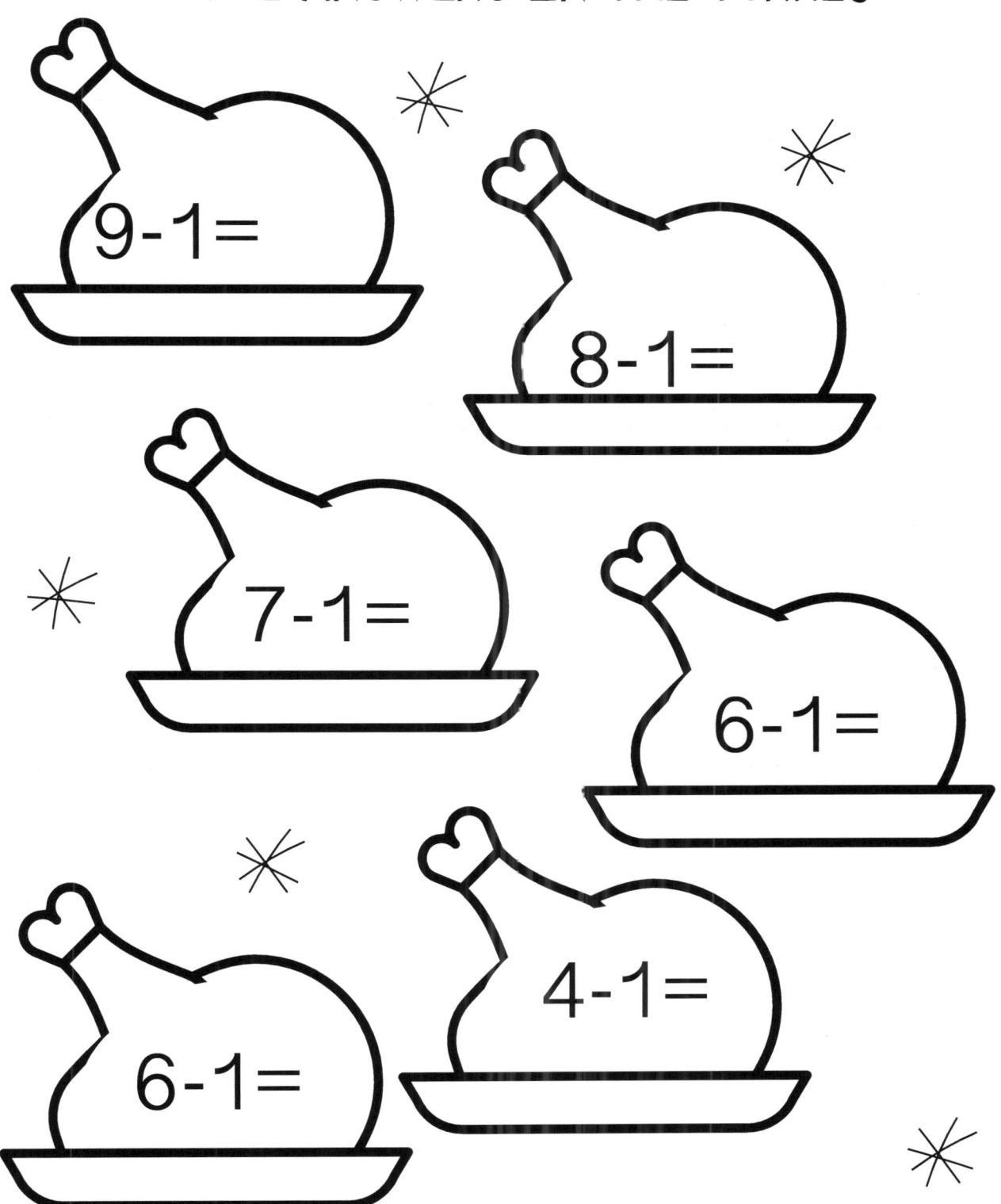

9-1=

8-1=

7-1=

6-1=

6-1=

4-1=

WHAT ARE YOU THANKFUL FOR?

LOOK FOR WORDS
PUMPKINS

PUP
_____

KIN
_____

_____

_____

_____

_____

_____

_____

CREATE WORD USING THE LETTERS
IN THE WORD GIVEN

WORD SEARCH

LOOK FOR THE WORDS RELATED TO THANKGIVING

```
T U R K E Y A S A L
L P I L G R I M D D
O H O M E A S I I I
V H O L I D A Y N N
E F E A S T A S E E
F A M I L Y A S A A
A S F H W E K R T
```

TURKEY   EAT   HOLIDAY

PILGRIM   FAMILY   HOME

FEAST   LOVE   DINE

COMPLETE THE SENTENCE

USE THE WORDS GIVEN TO FINISH THE SENTENCE

A KNIFE IS USED T CARVE THE _____.

AN _____ A DAY KEEPS THE DOCTOR AWAY.

A PUMKIN ___ TASTE YUMMY.

WIND RIPPLED THROUGH THE ___ FIELD

TURKEY   ACORN

PIE   APPLE

WORD SEARCH

T	H	A	N	K	A	S	A
H	S	T	H	A	N	K	R
A	T	H	A	N	K	S	W
N	A	T	H	A	N	K	S
K	W	R	T	H	A	N	K
E	A	T	H	A	N	K	S
W	T	H	A	N	K	S	A
E	A	S	D	E	J	R	T
R	T	T	H	A	N	K	A

LOOK FOR THE WORD 'THANK' THERE ARE 9 OF THEM

HELP THE PILGRIM!

HELP THE PILGRIM REACH THE BREAD

COUNT AND WRITE

COUNT THE NUMBER OF LEFT AND RIGHT LEAVES

LEFT

RIGHT

WHATS THE SUM?

10+10=

15+5=

12+10=

16+10=

19+10=

ADD THE NUMBERS AND WRITE THE SUM

WHAT AM I?

WRITE THE NAME OF THE DISH

DECODE MATH

🍐 + 🌰 = _____

🍐 + 🍐 = _____

🌰 + 🎃 = _____

🍎 + 🍎 = _____

🍐 =1   🌰 =2   🎃 =3   🍎 =4

USE THE PICTURE CODE TO SOLVE
THE MATH PROBLEM

FILL IN THE BLANK

USE THE VOWELS AND COMPLETE THE
WORDS THAT READ FROM LEFT TO RIGHT

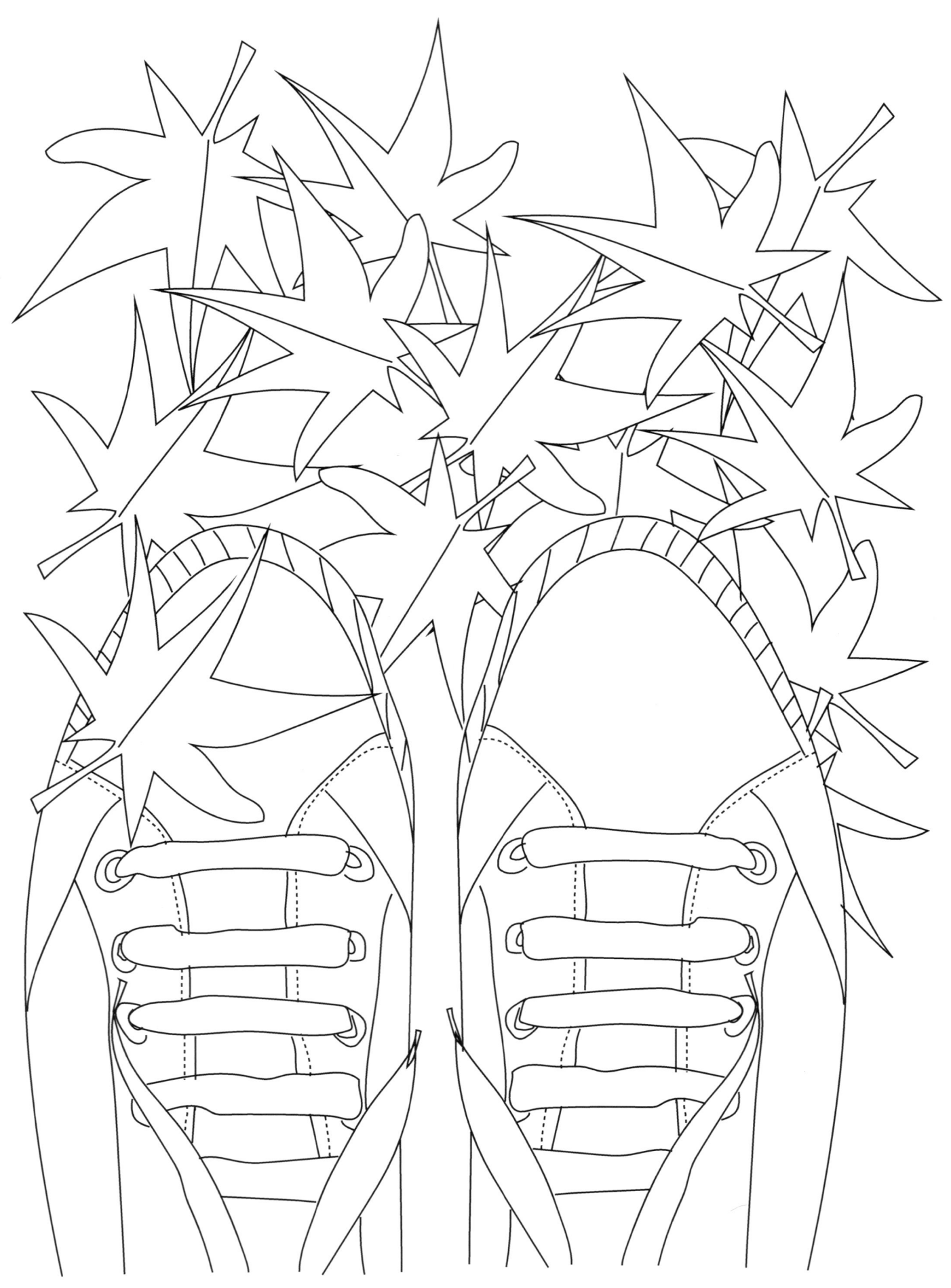

GREATER OR LESS THAN

203 ☐ 102

113 ☐ 113

213 ☐ 312

413 ☐ 410

103 ☐ 103

510 ☐ 500

SOLVE THE GREATER OR LESSER EQUATIONS
AND WRITE < , > OR =

PLACE VALUE
CIRCLE THE NUMBER IN THE ONES PLACE

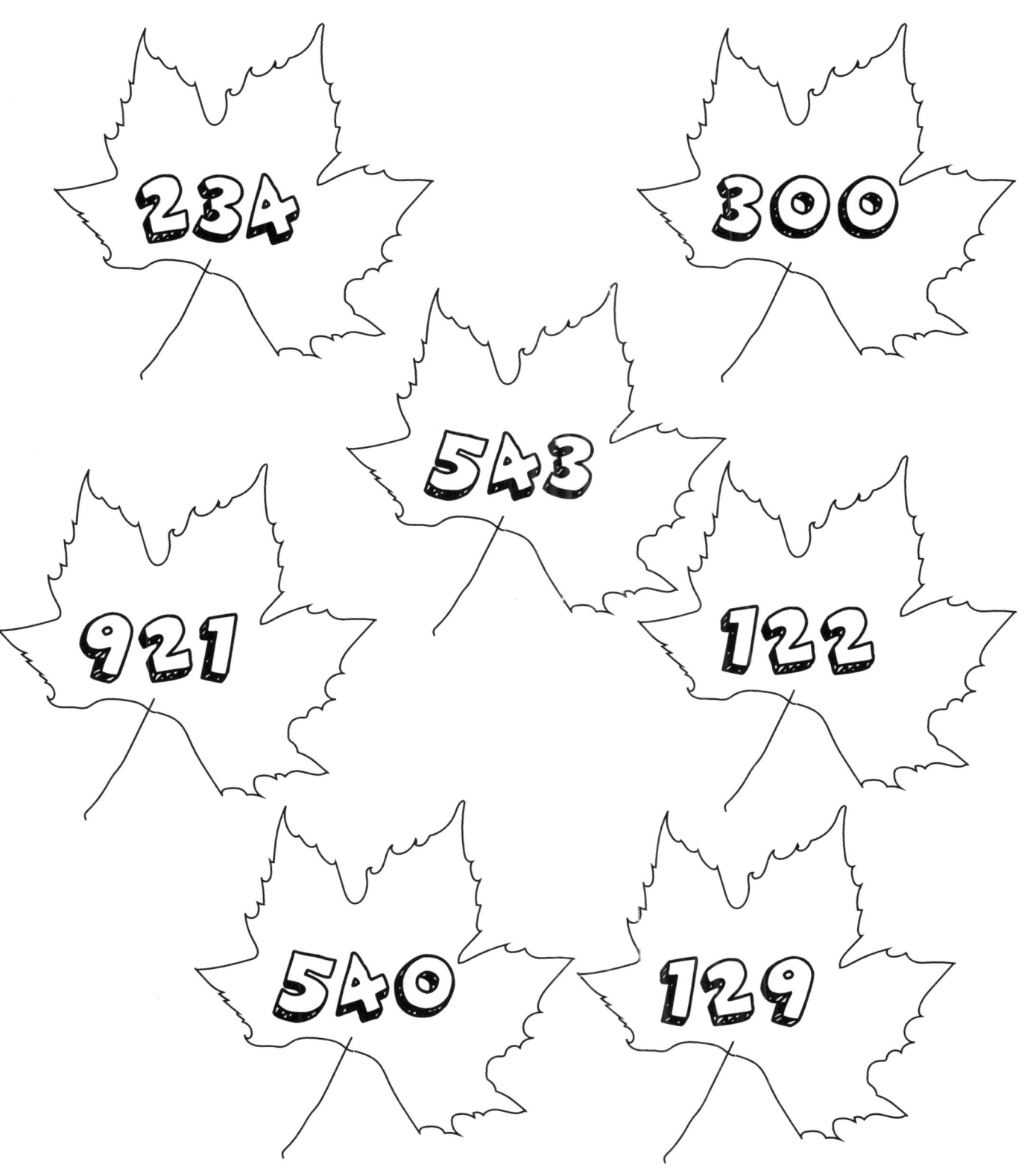

COMPLETE THE PATTERNS

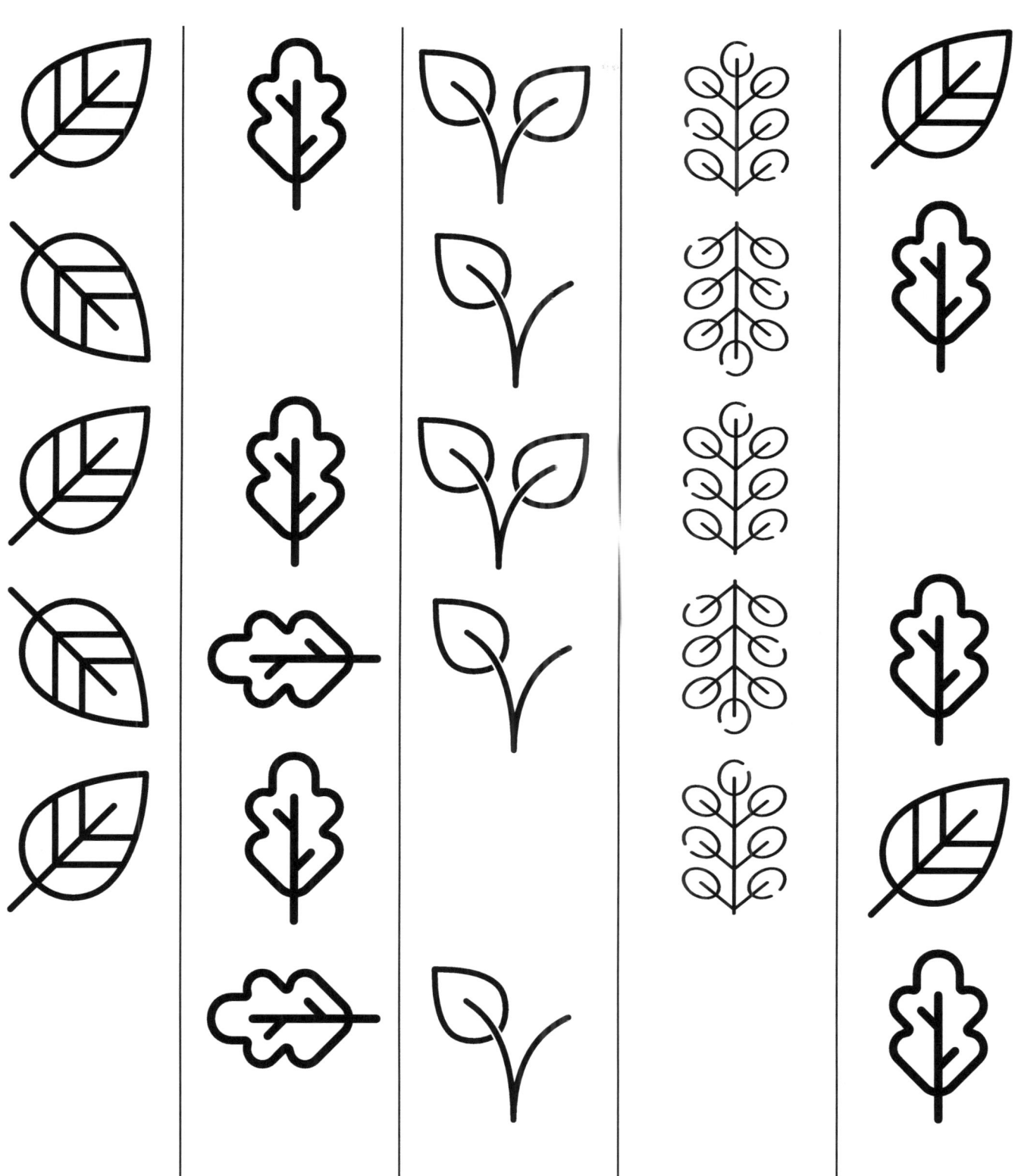

COMPLETE THE PATTERNS IN EACH ROW

CROSSWORD

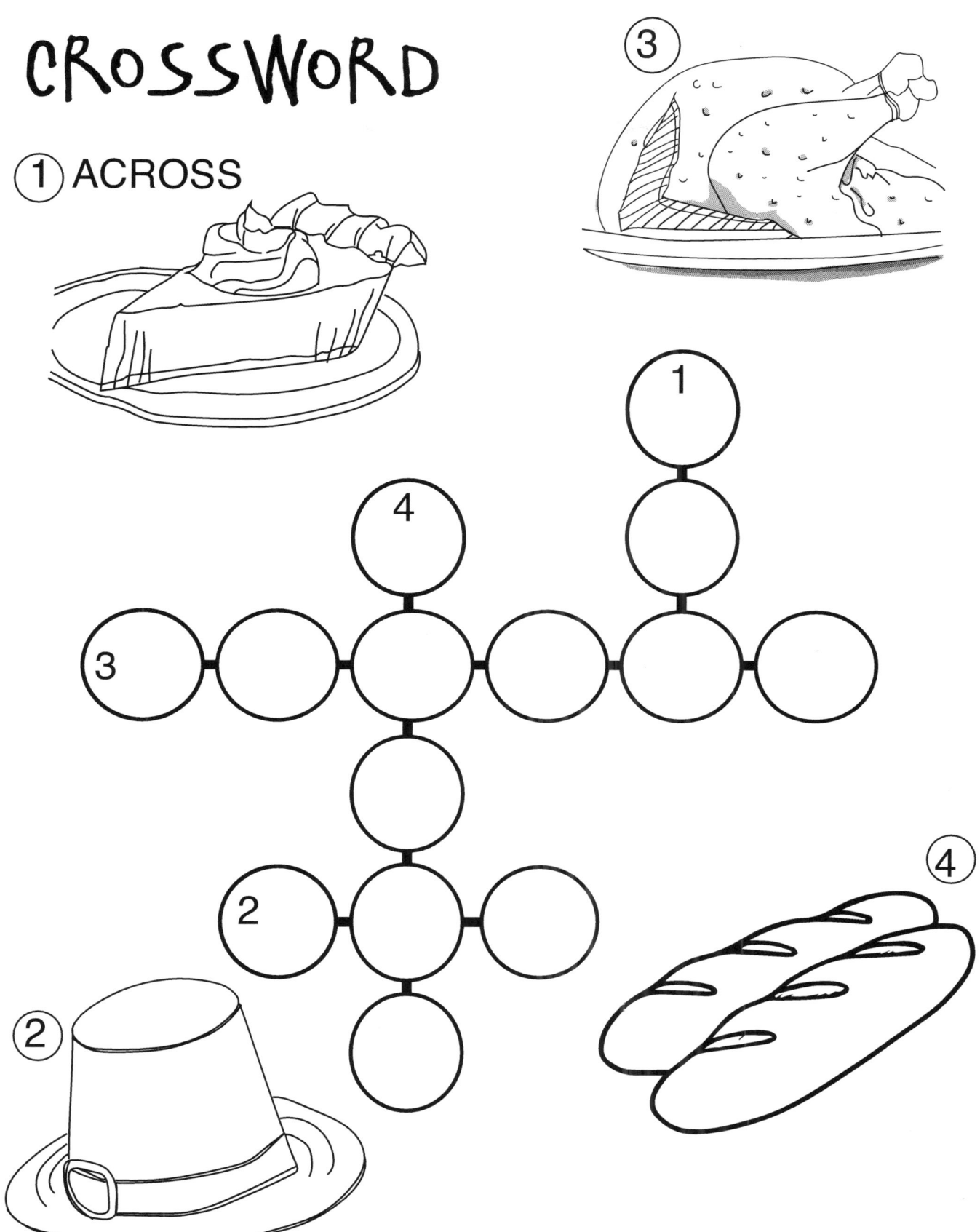

① ACROSS

SEE THE PICTURE AND WRITE THE WORDS
ASSOCIATED WITH THANKGIVING

JOIN THE DOTS

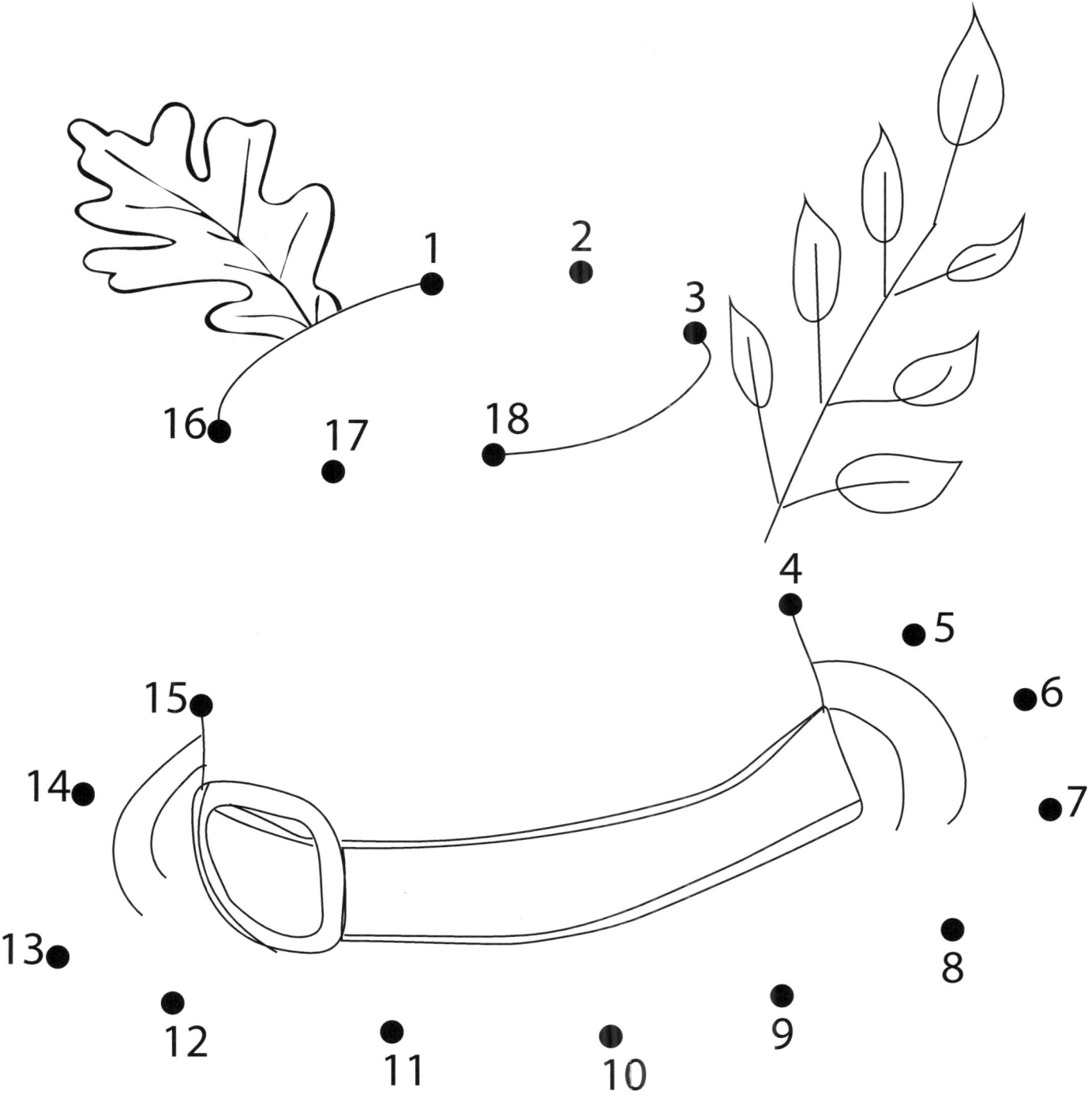

WHATS THE SUM?

ADD THE NUMBERS AND WRITE THE SUM IN THE SACK

3+10=

6+6=

11+5=

6+7=

9+4=

14+2=

MATCH THE FOLLOWING

FOOD

PILGRIM

HARVEST

LEAVES

MATCH THE PICTURES WITH THE WORD

JOIN THE DOTS

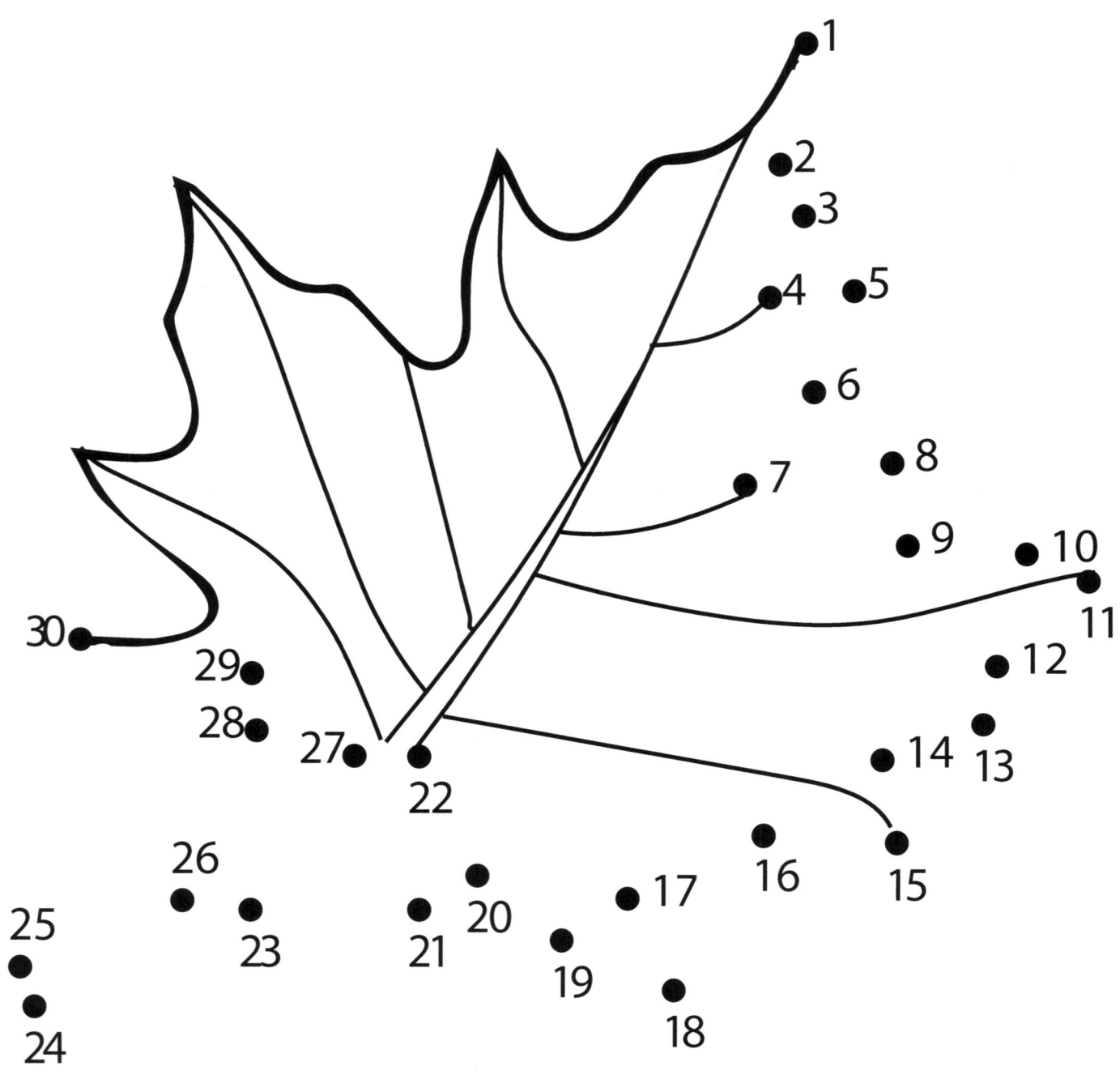

MATCH THE SHADOW

SELECT THE SHADOW THAT MATCHES THE TURKEY

GREATER OR LESS THAN

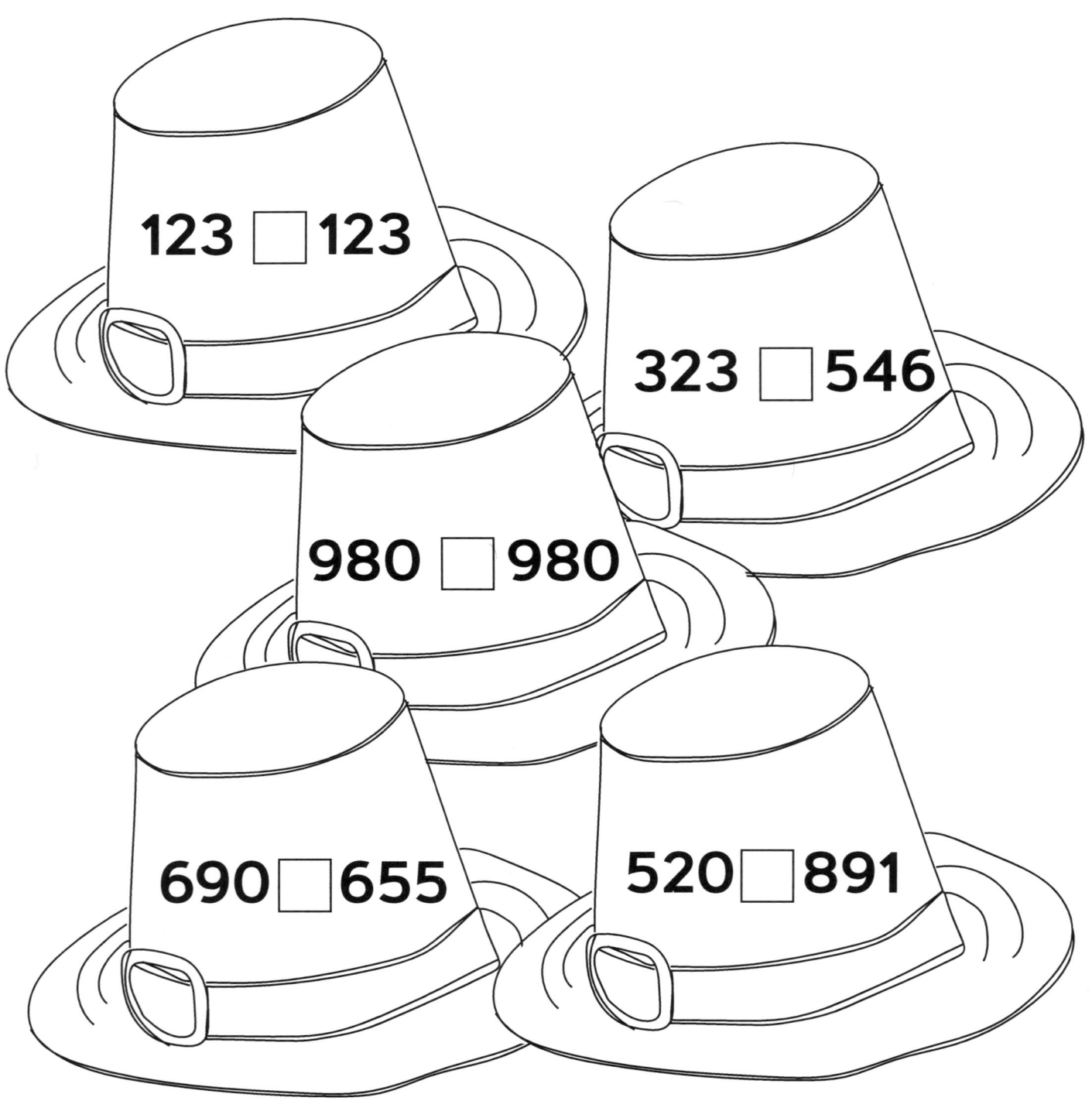

123 ☐ 123

323 ☐ 546

980 ☐ 980

690 ☐ 655

520 ☐ 891

SOLVE THE GREATER OR LESSER EQUATIONS
AND WRITE < , > OR =

COUNT AND WRITE

COUNT THE NUMBER OF LEFT AND RIGHT LEAVES

LEFT   RIGHT

WORD · SEARCH

LOOK FOR THE WORD 'LEAF' THERE ARE 10 OF THEM

FIND THE TRIPLETS

FIND AND CIRCLE THE THREE IDENTICAL PUMKINS

MATCH THE SHADOW

SELECT THE SHADOW
THAT MATCHES THE CORN

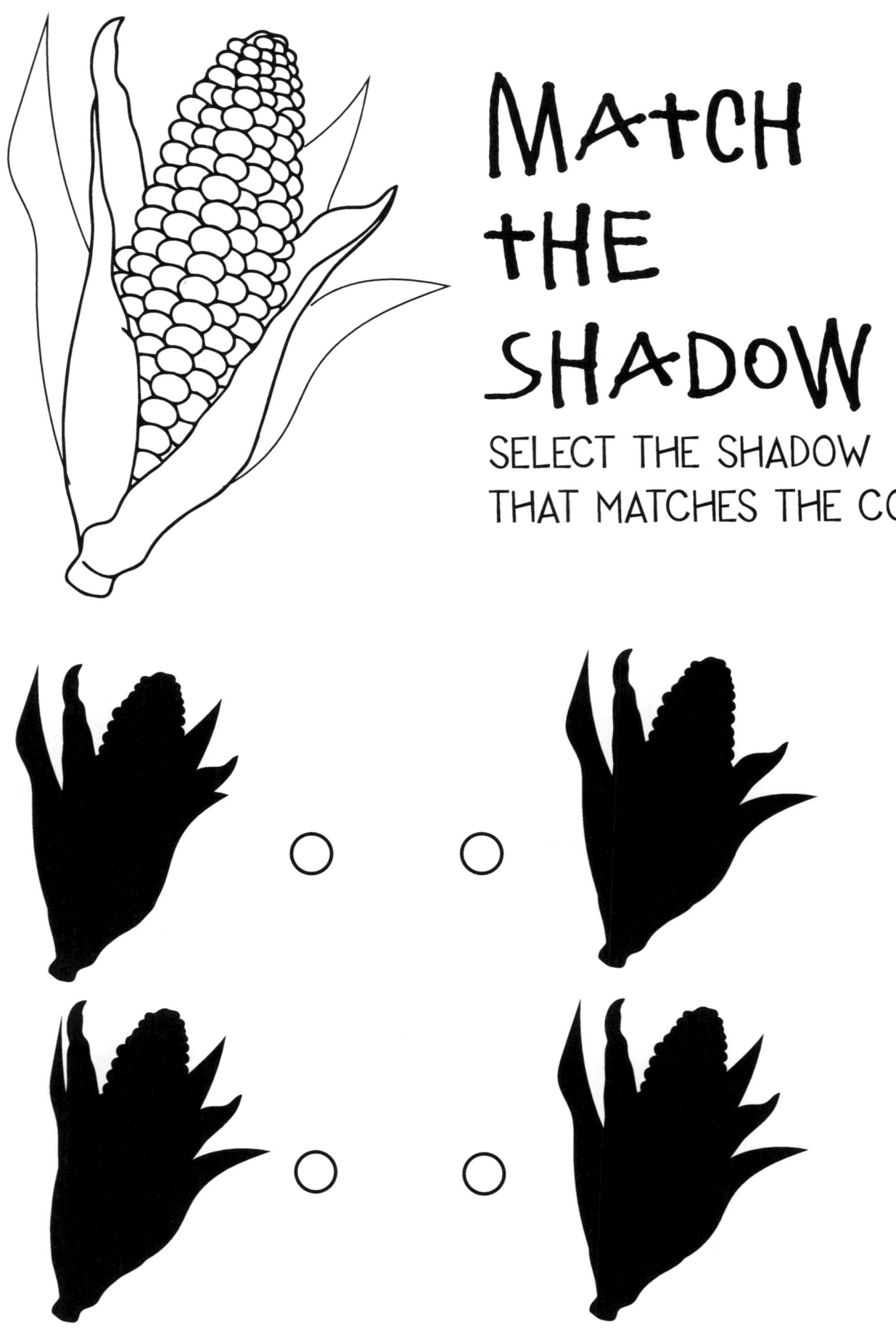

ALPHABETICAL ORDER

ARRANGE THE THANKGIVING RELATED WORDSI N ALPHABETICAL ORDER

PILGRIM

DINNER

TURKEY

THANK

PIE

HARVEST

LOVE

FAMILY

MEAL

EAT

1.

2.

3

4.

5.

6.

7.

8.

9.

10.

SPOT THE DIFFERENCE

SPOT AND CIRCLE THE 5 DIFFERENCES

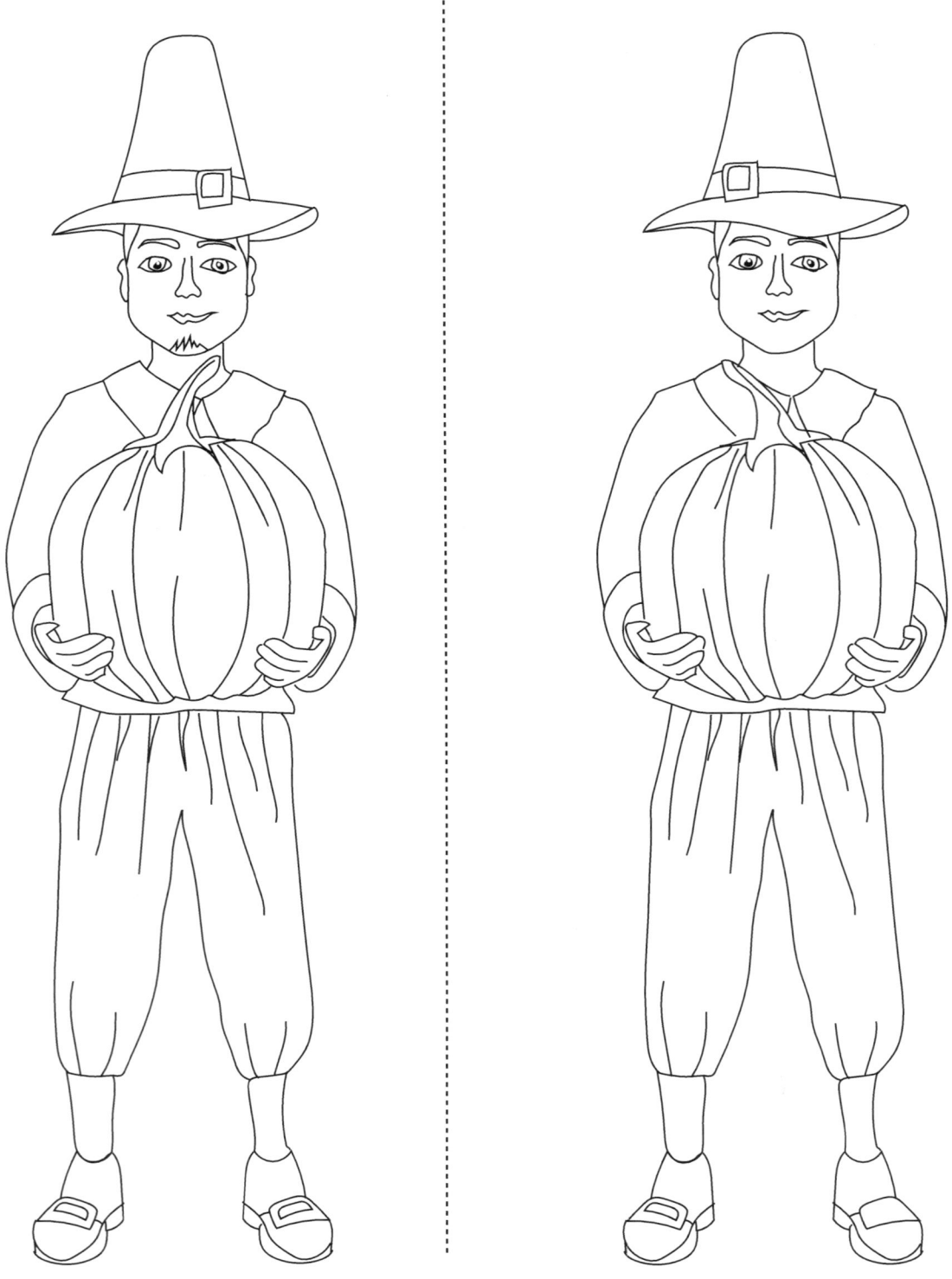

HELP THE SCARECROW!

HELP THE SCARECROW REACH THE CROW

CROW

COMPLETE THE PICTURE

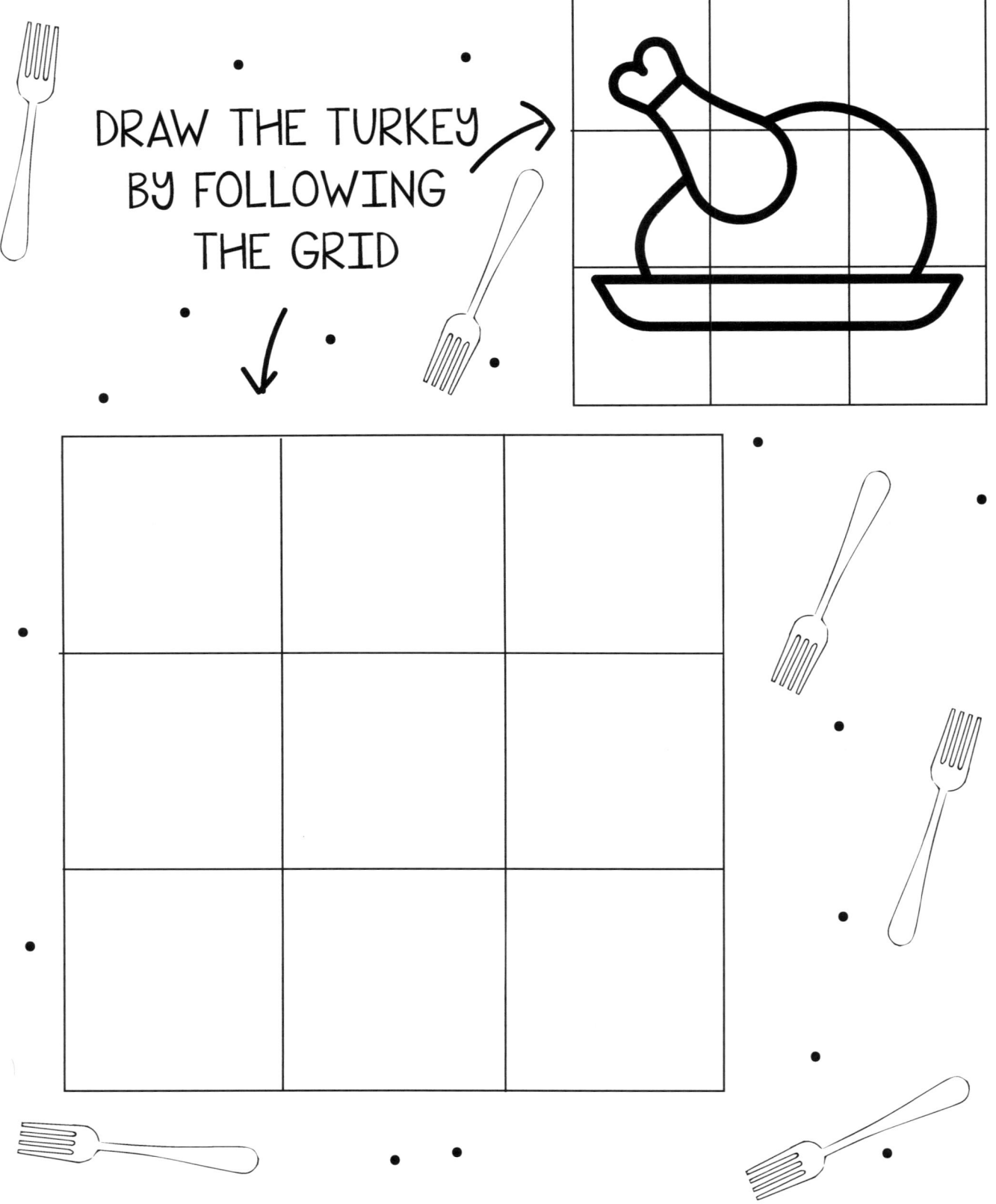

DRAW THE TURKEY
BY FOLLOWING
THE GRID

ALPHABETICAL ORDER

LEAF

FALL

AUTUMN

HAY

SQUASH

RAKE

GOURD

TREE

PUMPKIN

CORN

1.
2.
3
4.
5.
6.
7.
8.
9.
10.

ARRANGE THE AUTUMN RELATED WORDS
IN ALPHABETICAL ORDER

UNSCRAMBLE

REARRANGE THE LETTERS IN THE CORRECT ORDER
TO FIND THINGS RELATED TO THANKGIVING

PEI   _ _ _

 FSEAT   _ _ _ _ _ _

ETA   _ _ _

TKANH   _ _ _ _ _

 FYMILA   _ _ _ _ _ _

FDOO   _ _ _ _

 MLEA   _ _ _ _

DECODE MATH

🌿 + 🍃 =

_____

🌱 + 🌿 =

_____

🍃 + 🌱 =

_____

🍂 + 🍂 =

_____

🍃 =5   🌿 =2   🌱 =0   🍂 =4

USE THE PICTURE CODE TO SOLVE
THE MATH PROBLEM

SPOT THE DIFFERENCE

SPOT AND CIRCLE THE 5 DIFFERENCES

LOOK FOR WORDS
THANKGIVING

INK
_____

HAT
_____

_____

_____

_____

_____

_____

_____

CREATE WORD USING THE LETTERS
IN THE WORD GIVEN

FIND AND CIRCLE THE TWO IDENTICAL PILGRIMS

FIND THE tWINS

ODD ONE OUT

FIND THE PICTURE THAT DOES NOT
MATCH THE SET

COUNT AND DRAW

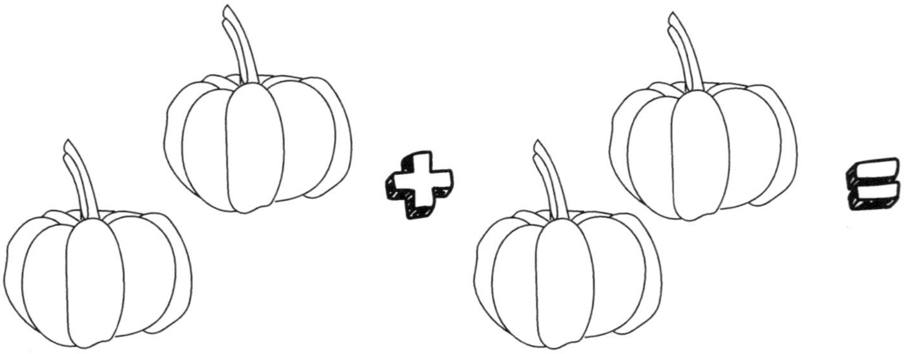

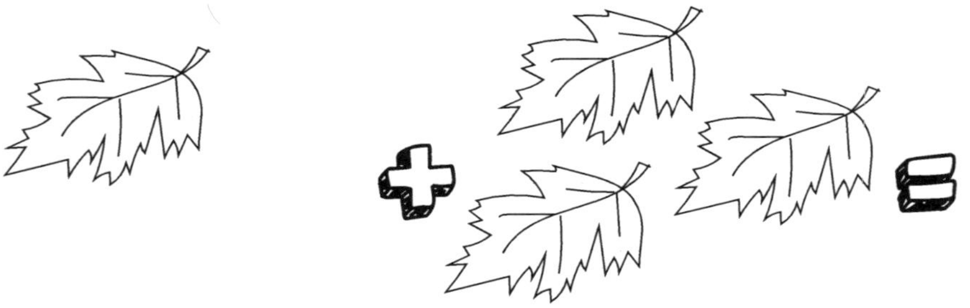

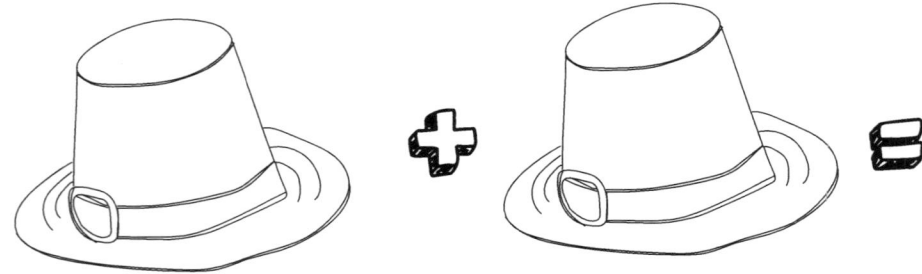

COUNT AND ADD, THEN DRAW THE NUMBER OF OBJECTS

MATCH THE HALF

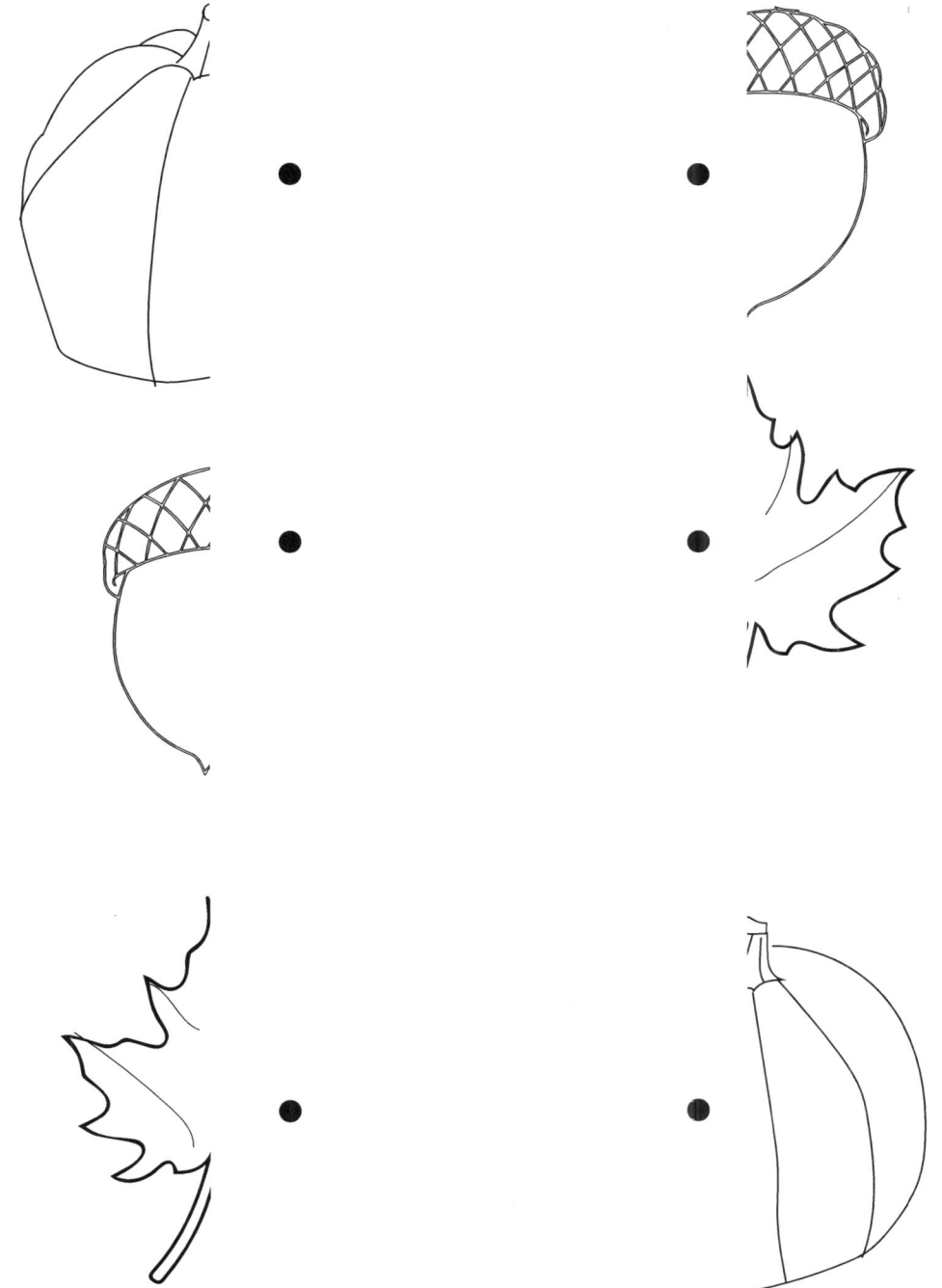

MATCH THE TWO HALVES OF THE IMAGES

SPOT THE DIFFERENCE
SPOT AND CIRCLE THE 5 DIFFERENCES

MATCH THE SHADOW

MATCH THE SHADOW WITH THE PICTURE

COMPLETE THE PATTERNS

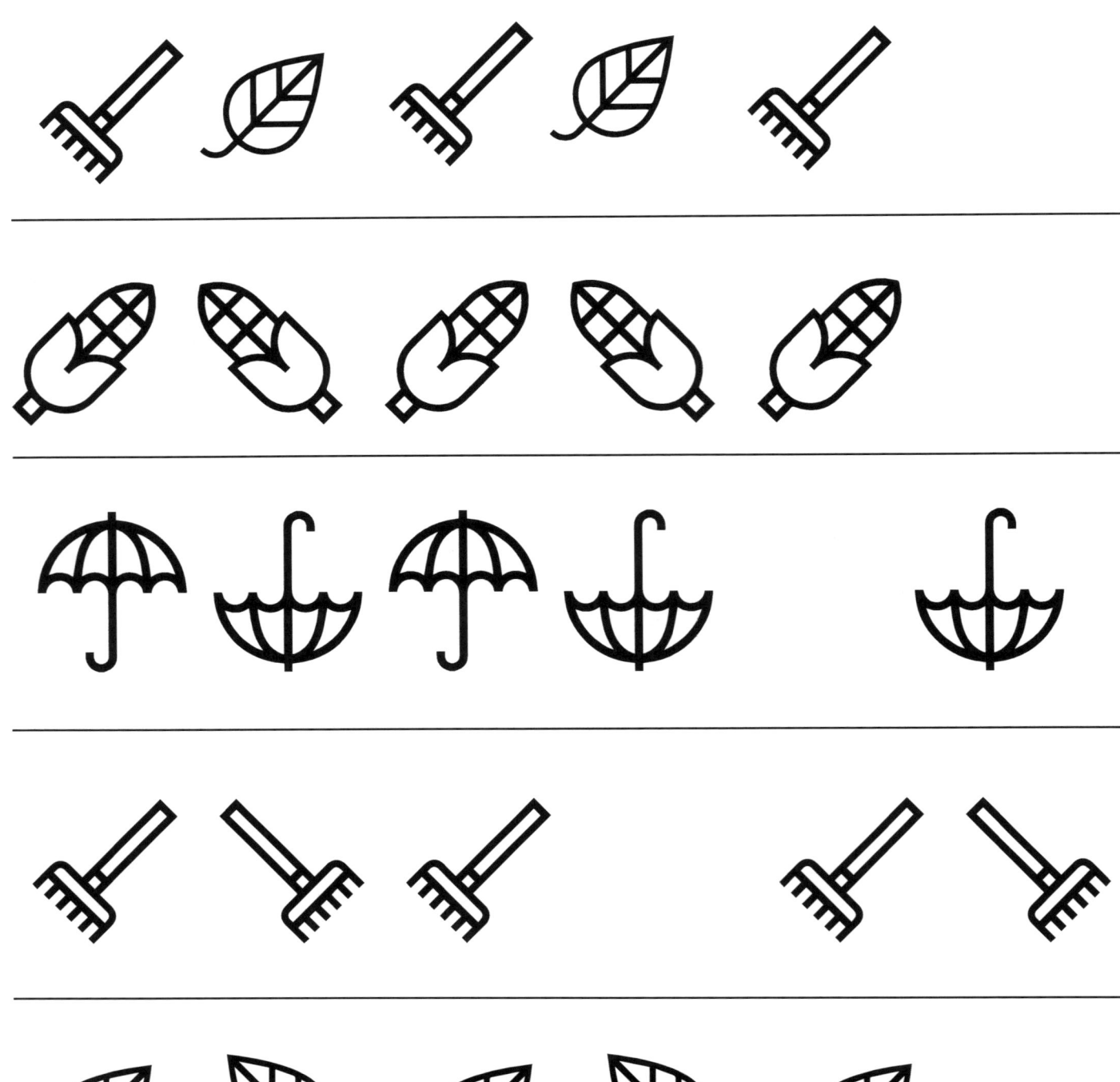

COMPLETE THE PATTERNS IN EACH ROW

MATCH THE HALF

MATCH THE TWO HALVES OF THE IMAGES

SPOT THE DIFFERENCE

SPOT AND CIRCLE THE 5 DIFFERENCES

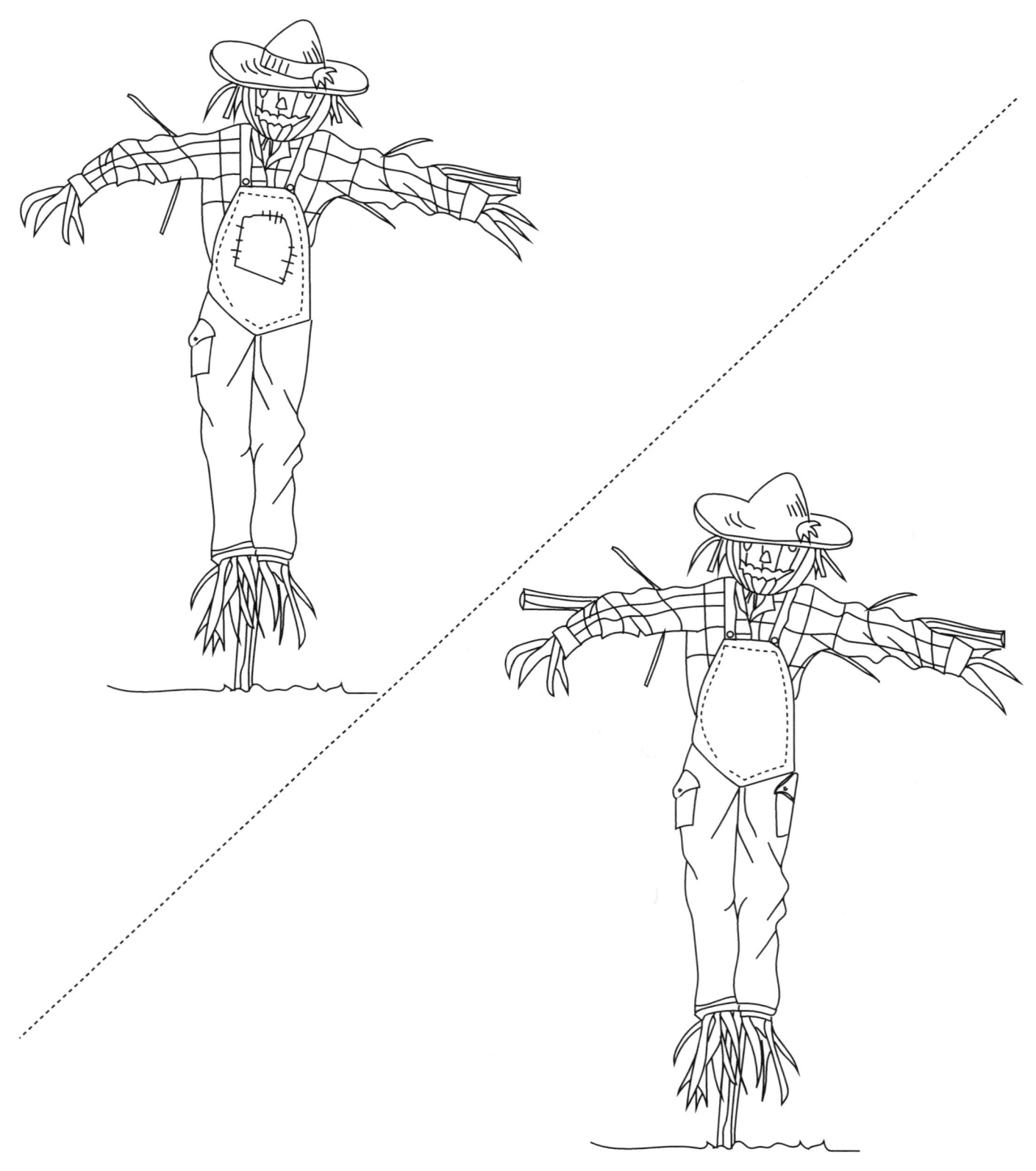

FILL THE NUMBERS
WRITE EACH OF THE MISSING NUMBERS

1 2 3 4 5 6 [ ]

8 [ ] 10 11 12 [ ]

14 [ ] 16 [ ] 18

19 [ ] 21 [ ] 23

24 [ ] 26 27 [ ]

COUNT AND DRAW

COUNT AND ADD, THEN DRAW THE NUMBER OF OBJECTS

EAT THE PIE!

FIND THE WAY FROM THE FORK TO THE PIE

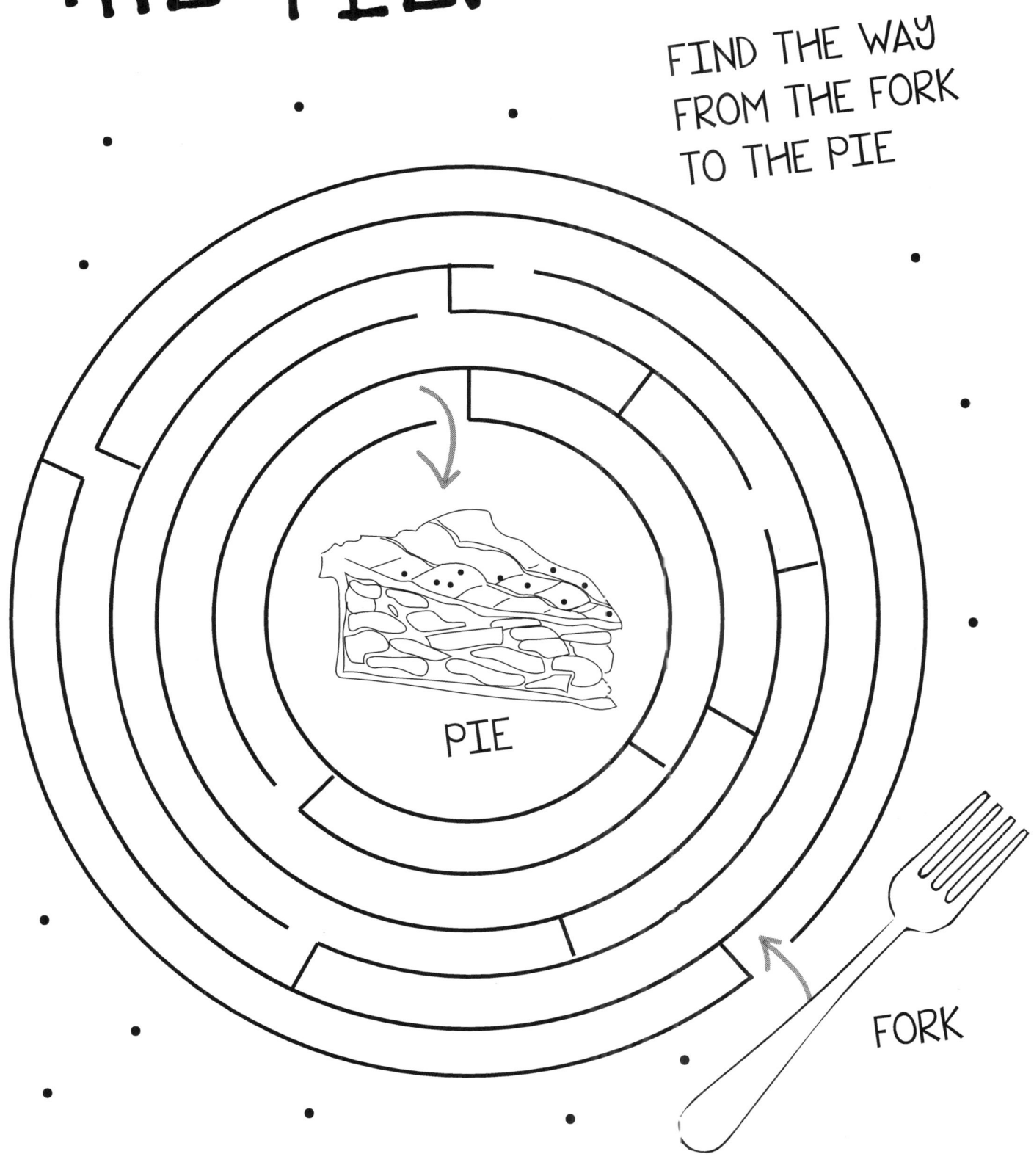

PIE

FORK

ODD ONE OUT

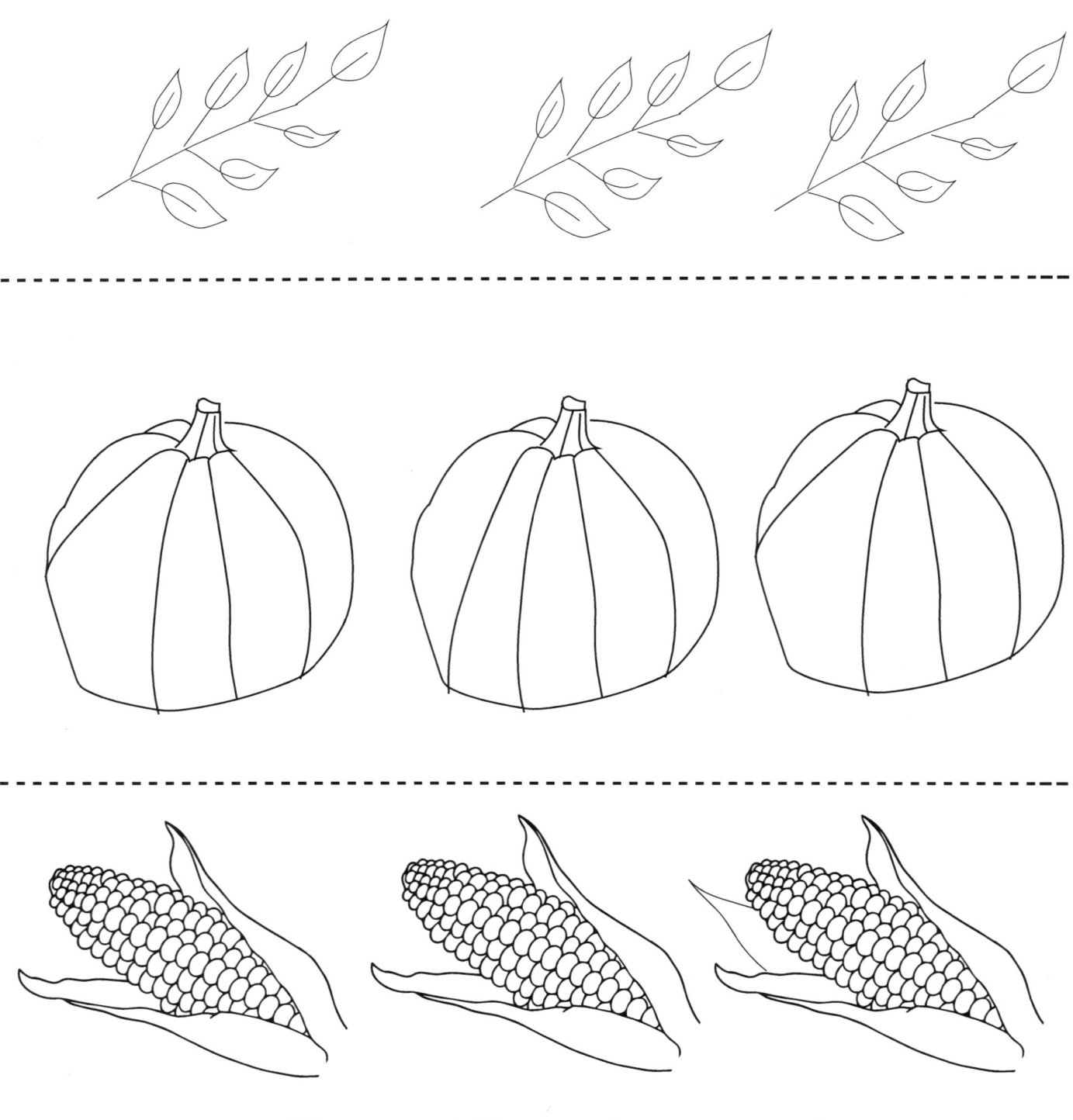

FIND THE PICTURE THAT DOES NOT
MATCH THE SET

FILL IN THE BLANK

A	C		R	N
C		R	V	
	P	P	L	
G	R		V	Y
B			N	S

A E I O U

USE THE VOWELS AND COMPLETE THE
WORDS THAT READ FROM LEFT TO RIGHT

Made in the
USA
Monee, IL